Mentorvention: Seize Control of Your Career With a Mentoring Intervention

Mentorvention: Seize Control of Your Career With a Mentoring Intervention

David Aron

Author's note: Most of the good people and supportive institutions in this book kept their names. If two or more people have the same name, I change names for clarity. The other ones get new names.

Introduction

On Monday morning, the start of only my fourth month at TechFirm (an early, early era online information provider), Tom walked over to my cubicle and sat himself down. "Tom! Welcome back. How was California?" I asked with genuine interest.

He leaned in, put his hand on my shoulder, grinned, and asked me, "Are you ready for this?"

Tom was one of three sales reps for our Ohio-based Electronic Shopper division of TechFirm. His job was to find new tenants for our revolutionary online shopping product, a shopping mall hosted entirely on the TechFirm platform. By tenants, I mean merchants and businesses, both brick-and-mortar and online only, that would try to sell their offerings through our online shopping service. And by revolutionary, I mean that in 1989, online shopping was a fantasy only for the most dedicated computer users. And in 1989, there weren't very many computer users. I had somehow stumbled out of my first job, 80-store shopping mall management with a boss stuck in the stone age, right onto the cutting edge of consumer technology.

Tom had just returned from a trip out west to meet a few of our current clients (mall tenants) and sweet talk some prospective mall stores. I anticipated some good news. Tom could even make bad news seem good. Tom was a fine salesman. "We closed on 'Haight of Suspense,' that bookstore in San Francisco." Tom held out his hand to count, "They're going live in two weeks with a grand opening, a write-up in our print magazine, a contest, and a live interactive author interview session. That's no problem for you, right?"

In order to close the deal with a prospect, or re-sign a returning mall store, promises had to be made. This was a scary new world for everyone involved, and we needed our partners to be confident we knew what we were doing and that we would help them succeed in this unfamiliar environment. And then when the deal was done, it was my job to make all of those promises come true. But this was a lot to ask. "Two weeks?" I was surprised. "Usually the turnaround is two months! And they want what?"

"Well," Tom replied. "Mandy told them you would make it happen."

Mandy. I closed my eyes and threw my head back. Just hearing Mandy's name was a punch to the gut. Mandy was a tornado, a seductress, and Pandora's box all wrapped in one. She was our creative consultant, based in New York and brought along by our sales reps to help close some of our more challenging and lucrative contracts. She could effortlessly come up with amazing, fantastical ideas and sell them to clients who absolutely jumped on board and wanted more. And she would always come up with more.

With several dozen vendors in our Electronic Shopper, our coders and account support team had their collective hands full on a daily basis. There were certainly bigger clients that demanded and deserved extra attention. But this book store wasn't going to be one of them. Yet there we were. The sales reps appreciated Mandy because she made the promises that helped them close their deals. The rest of us? Me, the coders, the account support team? Well, Mandy happened to be best friends with Ronnie, our department Director (our mall

Introduction

manager's boss). Mandy was bulletproof. Nobody wanted to be on Mandy's bad side. And dissent was not appreciated. Could my boss, our mall manager, help?

What mall manager? The creator of our Electronic Shopper, Jim, the visionary who brought me to TechFirm (you might say rescued me from my awful prior job), was fired a month prior, the week before Christmas. Jim was daring, thrilling, inspiring, and I hoped I could learn from him. Nope. The new mall manager, Ted, was just brought in two weeks earlier. Ted was the opposite of Jim and would not challenge his boss – Mandy's best friend.

That punch to the gut I mentioned earlier was a monthly event for me, whenever Mandy would come to Ohio for her regular consulting visit. Those were days I dreaded. I wouldn't fall asleep the night before, struggled to get dressed in the morning, and spent the days feeling stress, inadequacy, anger, and resentment. My stomach hurts just writing about it. And Mandy, with all of her promises and creativity and invulnerability, probably didn't know and certainly didn't care. She just inadvertently made sure I was stuck where I was, in a job I didn't recognize surrounded by people who weren't really quite sure what I was supposed to be doing there anyway. Sometimes, I didn't even know what I was doing there anymore. Why did she keep doing this to me?

Well, it really wasn't her fault that four months into my second job, after a miserable year at my first job, after I followed my wife to Ohio and went to get my MBA because I had no idea what to do with my bachelor's degree in psychology and didn't know how to conduct a proper job search, I was lost and miserable. I was 25 years old and my career was already out of control. I didn't even know what a career or control looked like. My life was careening and spinning, without my hands anywhere close to the steering wheel. I could have used some help. Some wisdom. I could have used a mentor. But I didn't have one and wasn't even aware of what a mentor was at the time. Through this book, I hope you won't find yourself in that same situation.

***

My friends, that was quite a few years ago.

I still think about Mandy and Tom, Jim and Ronnie, Ted, and that whole cast of characters. I think of my brick-and-mortar boss and his boss too. All these experiences, good and bad and worse and better, they combined to bring me to where I am today. And that has worked out just fine. Today, I am finally in control of my career. I have my hands firmly on the wheel.

How about you?

Where are you today?

Where will you be tomorrow?

Are you in control of your career?

If you are not sure of the answers to any of those questions, or worse, you don't like the answers, you are not alone. But the good news is you can take back control of your life and career just like I did. By learning from the good and bad of my experiences you can do it in a fraction of the time. And if you are in a place where those answers are solidly affirmative, my hope is you can use this book to pay it forward and learn how to help share your own journey with those you encounter who may need it the most.

Introduction

When I speak to students, alumni, and clients about their careers, I ask them how they deal with their challenges at work. Here are some of the things they tell me:

- I just ask my boss
- Sometimes I'll just text my friend and we'll complain to each other
- I don't really have one approach, I just deal with it

When I bring up the topic of mentors and mentoring experiences, I get comments like this:

- I don't have one
- I wish I had one
- I was matched with a mentor at work but we never see each other

And one that makes me especially sad, that I've heard multiple times in different ways:

I had a mentor but they just kind of screwed me over and took credit for my work

We all want greater control over our careers. You just saw how much I needed to gain some sort of control. I'll have a few more stories like that to share with you. The best way to gain control over your career is by working with a mentor. Comments like the ones you just read might make you think working with a mentor isn't easy or isn't such a good idea. But it can be. **Finding and working with a mentor is a good idea and you should have a relationship with one or more mentors right now to help you gain control over your career.** The key is to find the *right* mentors. And to be the right kind of protégé or mentee.

You know the old question: "If you could, what advice would you give to your past self?"

Here's a better question: "If you could, what advice would you want to hear from your future self?"

Think of a mentor as a version of your future self. Someone who has already seen a lot of the things you are now dealing with.

I wish someone had told me to think about that 38 years ago.

And again 35 years ago.

And again 20 years ago.

Can you even imagine who your future self is, and what they would possibly want to tell you?

Here's where I can help. This book is about mentoring. In some ways, that might make me a mentor to you, a role I gladly accept. I'm sure many of my experiences present lessons that are valuable to you. Then again, many might not be. You'll have to create your own group of advisors, a shopping cart of mentors and relationships you fill to help you stay in control of your career. You will have to develop mentoring relationships the right way. That's what this book is about. **Gaining control over your career by creating an ideal set of mentoring relationships.**

I've worked as a teacher and mentor for thousands of students and advisees, dozens and dozens of entrepreneurs and clients over the 30 or so years since I left TechFirm (in case you were wondering how I finally dealt with my Mandy situation... along with another, more dramatic reason for me to leave that I'll tell you about later) and entered academia – and ultimately coaching.

Introduction

Before that, and even during that, I was the one who needed a mentor. That's something I didn't know then but I know it now. I wish my future self could have told me that. But he didn't.

Good mentors can be hard to find.

But guess what? Good mentees, or protégés, can also be hard to find.

This book will help you find a good mentor and establish satisfying, productive relationships with mentors covering a number of areas in your career and in your life. A lot of that comes from helping you to become the kind of person a mentor wants to work with, and THAT comes from helping you understand how much you have to offer in that kind of relationship.

In case you missed that last line, I'll say it again. You have a lot to offer.

And this book is NOT about "fake it 'til you make it."

It IS about "be it and you'll see it."

And so will those around you.

This book is meant for people like you, people who want to gain control over their careers, like me from back when I was spinning out of control – during and after my MBA, during and after my shopping mall job, during and after my TechFirm job, during and after my first academic job that did not last – all these different pivotal stages of my career I experienced in my mid-20s, my early 30s, and my early 40s.

This book is for you.

Chapter 1: I Feel Like I Have No Control

In the introduction, I shared with you the challenges I faced in my second job, soon after my demoralizing first job. This situation highlighted a recurring theme in my early career: a lack of control. My coworker, Mandy, made unrealistic promises to clients all in the name of closing the deal, making the sale without considering the workload it would create. Our new manager, Ted, wouldn't challenge Mandy due to her close friendship with his boss. I felt stuck and utterly unable to influence the situation. Even though I experienced these episodes years ago, many common elements relating to lack of control might seem very familiar to you: people, conflict, miscommunication, and unrealistic or poorly expressed expectations. I'll share more details about these stories with you and then talk about the actual outcomes, what I should have done, and how a mentor would have helped.

Early Days

My first full time job, even before my job at TechFirm, came a few months after I earned my MBA at The Ohio State University. This was in 1988, shortly after a historical stock market crash in 1987 which meant all the jobs, including the marketing jobs, seemed to be going to the finance students. I might have been wrong but that's how it felt to the half dozen or so of us marketing students who met frequently on campus to check the job boards and share our tales of jobless woe. In that era, the classic tools of the job search like networking existed, but I didn't know how to use them. I relied on the print newspaper "help wanted ads," and that's where I saw a job opening that sounded perfect: shopping mall management!

The shopping mall seeking an assistant manager was called Eastland, located on the east side of Columbus, Ohio. And in my role as assistant mall manager, I would be responsible for promoting the mall and its 80 tenants. Perfect! That made so much sense since I enjoyed retail and studied marketing. The ad also clearly stated an MBA was required, and I had a brand new one! I think they wanted some experience too, which at that point I lacked. But I got the job.

Unfortunately, the reality of working at the shopping mall was far from ideal. My immediate supervisor was the mall general manager named Whit, and his boss, the regional manager, was Pablo. These grown men (Whit was around 40, Pablo in his 60s) were constantly butting heads. Whit was "By The Book" and felt any idea, any creativity, was just a waste of money and a wasted effort that would only serve to attract non-shoppers. Pablo, his boss, was "By The Seat of His Pants." He was wildly creative (an attribute often fueled by his long liquid lunches off-site) and loved every idea he had and every idea he heard. This created a chaotic environment where I was stuck in the middle. Literally, our offices were lined up in a row and there was no avoiding it: They bombarded me with conflicting requests and instructions, leaving me feeling powerless.

One early example exemplifies my lack of control. Two months into my year at Eastland, the regional manager, Pablo, was fixated on the brown winter grass around the exterior of the mall and believed it detracted from the shopping experience. His solution was to have me tell our maintenance crew to spray paint the mall grass green. That's right, spray paint the grass surrounding a shopping mall in November so it looked better. And I, as a recent graduate with a pregnant wife and limited career experience, felt immense pressure to follow orders. Relaying this absurd request to the maintenance crew, I was met with a wave of laughter and general disrespect. Something tells me they might have heard this kind of thing before.

My initial attempt at asserting myself crumbled. Nervous and caught in the middle, I sheepishly reinforced the order. Thankfully, the situation took an unexpected turn. Our Sears store, the only place in the mall that had a paint department, had only a limited supply of green spray paint. The crew used the few available cans to paint a small patch of grass right outside of Pablo's office window, and it was never brought up again. And yet somehow things got worse.

Among my responsibilities for my boss, Whit, was serving as his article clipping service. Why not Google? Remember, this was the late 1980s, and the nearest computer was on the other side of the mall, for sale inside our Radio Shack store. And computers were not in our budget. So I would read through and gather articles from retail and shopping center trade papers as well as fashion magazines and other publications related to our stores. I'd find interesting articles, tear them out, write a few words on a little Post-It note, clip the articles together, and leave them on the boss's desk if his door was open, or leave them on our (shared) secretary Lena's desk if his door was closed.

One evening, I was the last one in the office, hurrying to close up and get home. I remember not being able to find a paperclip and was too eager to go home to bother searching for one, so I just left a pile of articles, neatly stacked, on our secretary's desk. The article on top of the stack was from a fashion magazine with the headline that read something along the lines of "Career Women: How to Dress in the '90s." The notes stuck on that article and each of the others had a few words about the content and for which of our stores it might be a good conversation starter. And on the very top, stuck right under the headline for the article on top of the pile about how women should dress for success, was a kind of summary note that simply said, "You should read these."

The next morning, Lena got to work and saw the pile. She saw the note on top of the pile. She saw the headline. I can only imagine the first thought in her head was, "Here's this new guy and HE'S telling ME how I should dress?"

You might be wondering why Lena thought this was about her, especially since this was not the first time I had left such a stack of articles on her desk, clearly intended for our boss. Keep on wondering… I'm still wondering too. Whatever work Lena had done for me the day before (answered the phone and took a message, I think?) became the last thing she would ever do for me. I'm not exaggerating. No typing. No filing. No calls. No messages. She just wouldn't do it. Total shut down for the remaining 9 months or so I was there. That's not how things are supposed to work!

Whit did nothing about it, despite my complaints. Pablo did nothing either, and realistically, he shouldn't have had to. Now on the other hand, Pablo's secretary, Sharon, was quite sympathetic to my plight. Perhaps years of working for Pablo had taught her everybody makes embarrassing mistakes, even if that person is not ready to admit they made one. Sharon took my calls and basically worked as my secretary when she had the time. But Pablo kept her pretty busy with his regional management responsibilities and the need to occasionally clean up his messes. Essentially, everybody noticed Lena had stopped working for me, despite her job description. Nobody did anything. And it went on like that for nine months.

The Only Constant is Change

One more story and then we'll talk about what we can learn from all this. For this one, we need to jump ahead ten years, past Lena, over Mandy, through TechFirm, and beyond graduate school and my major career change. We'll talk about all that soon enough. Let's go to Chicago and my very first day at Chicagoland University, where I was elated to have my first university job. That was my big career change, from industry to academia. I was born in Chicago and lived in the Chicago area for the first 22 years of my life. Even my undergraduate school was Northwestern University, just north of the city. Then, I got married. My wife and I, and then our children, spent the next twelve years in Ohio and then Michigan. So getting a job at a Chicago school and moving back home seemed too good to be true. And you know what that means.

My first day at my new job included a full department meeting with all my fellow marketing professors, about two dozen people in all. Chet, who at the time was the department chair, started the meeting by introducing the new hires (including me) and continued by making two big announcements. First, Chet told us we were starting a formal mentoring program, in which the newest junior faculty (in our first, second, or third years) were to be matched with a team of three senior marketing faculty members. You could almost see the vapor trails as senior faculty members pushed themselves away from the table. It was to be a formal mentoring program and the mentors did not want to play. Good mentors are hard to find.

David Aron

Also at this meeting, the Chair made his second big announcement: our department was transitioning from being focused on teaching to becoming a department more focused on research. Quick side note: college departments and their faculty in any specialty focus on teaching or research. Sometimes both. And sometimes more of one than the other. Some almost to the minimization or exclusion of the other. Chicagoland was closer to a teaching focus, or so I thought until that afternoon. After the meeting, I joined the other new professors for a drink and all I remember is staring out the window realizing that after only one day, this was no longer the job I was hired for. What a miserable way to start a new job, the job I thought would be a perfect fit, starting my new career in my old home town. That day really set the tone for the next six years.

Now on the surface, an academic's demands seem pretty simple. Teach well and create knowledge. The create knowledge part, for a marketing professor, means publishing academic articles about marketing research in academic journals, to be read by other marketing professors. The teaching part, I did well enough. The research part, I did not. After five years I had published only one such research article. That is objectively not enough, not even close for a research-leaning department like mine. Susan, the department chair who replaced Chet, gently let me know I should not bother going up for tenure (the brass ring so many professors chase) because there was no way I would earn that prize. Better to say I never tried than tried and failed. I don't know if that was good advice or not. I received a lot of bad advice during my years at Chicagoland, which will come up again later. But in the end, she was right. Chicagoland's demands were pretty simple and I did not meet them. I didn't know how and I didn't know what to do next.

Learn From Your Mistakes

To recap, in the first 10 years of my career I left one awful job, left another miserable job, changed careers and earned a PhD, and then got fired from my third job which was also awful and miserable. Funny how the common factor here seems to be me. But here's what I learned:

In all three of these jobs, something broke and I didn't fix it.

With Lena at Eastland Mall, I didn't fix our broken relationship. Whether I broke it or she did, this misunderstanding, this relationship, was never repaired. You can bet I blamed my boss, Whit, for this. With Mandy at TechFirm, we never had a relationship. She was something that happened to me. You can bet I blamed Mandy for this. Yet considering the impact her actions had on my work and beyond that, I took no action. I only reacted. Ultimately, if something affects me, I'm the one who needs to fix it. Proactively, not reactively.

This is a good time to revisit the question I raised in the introduction. What advice would you give to your past self? My past self made those mistakes and didn't fix his problems. That's why I like the other question better. What advice would you want from your future self?

Consider a mentor as a version of your future self. There were no mentors for me at the mall. Let me correct that. There were more than 80 store managers of varying degrees of experience, wisdom, and willingness to share at that mall, every day of the week. I can think of a handful right now I might have talked to for advice. Instead, my mind was filled with Whit's attitude that we and our store managers had relationships made of daily conflict and limited resources. And there I go, blaming someone else for my problems. So here's another lesson: show yourself some grace. I was a 24-year-old kid with little experience and less perspective.

At TechFirm, I can think of several people who I might have reached out to for mentorship. The situation was peculiar in that my hiring itself seemed to be a bit on the fringes of the normal standard operating procedure. Jim, the guy who hired me, was thrilled about my brick-and-mortar mall experience. He warned me, though, that my one year of experience would be a stumbling block when it came to our human resources department and coached me in ways to communicate the quality of my experience over the quantity. So Jim, he might have been a mentor, a guide to my future, if only he hadn't been fired so soon after I started. And why didn't I keep in touch with Jim? That is a really good question. I guess I didn't know I could. I really had no idea what building a network meant. Other than Jim, there were a few people in the company, but not my department, I could have sought out. So I guess I'd tell my past self to be more proactive in seeking relationships with possible mentors.

But my future self has a few other ideas. Like how my issues with Lena, Mandy, and Chet all happened within the first few months (or in Chet's case, hours) of my first, second, and third jobs, respectively. And I haven't had any Lenas, Mandys, or Chet's since then. This was quite a revelation I only recently experienced. Does that mean there are no more Lenas, Mandys, or Chet's? Of course not. In fact, since you're reading this, I'm sure you have at least one of these characters or variations of them in your life, with their own names and your own challenges. On the other hand, I think a few years of bumps and bruises, not to mention the many courses on marketing I've taught and on management I've taken, have helped me learn a few lessons about power.

Control vs Power

We don't have to get into the semantics, the differences between "control" and "power" here. If you feel powerless, you feel like you have no control. And a new person on the job is going to be lacking in both power and control. We're talking about the same thing here. But not all power is created equal, nor does it impact different people in the same way. To better understand how these power dynamics can impact you, let's look at how they played out in my own story.

Legitimate Power

Legitimate power is your boss. Their boss. Your CEO. Somebody who, by virtue of their title or rank, has authority over others. Legitimate power refers to the influence someone has based on their position or title within a hierarchy or organizational chart. In my experience, Whit the mall manager held legitimate power over me. Pablo held legitimate power over both Whit and me, because of their formal roles in the organization. This power comes from the acceptance of a hierarchy, where people in higher positions are seen as having the authority to make decisions and give directions to those lower in the hierarchy. In my TechFirm story, Mandy did not have this sort of power but her best friend Ronnie did. At Chicagoland, and academics in general, the relationship is less clear and we'll explore that more in a moment for those who have careers in that industry. And back to the shopping mall, my relationship with Lena is even less clear, because formally speaking, she reported to Whit, not to me, even though her job description suggested she would also do the work I asked her to do. Which she did not.

Coercive Power

This is not as clearly spelled out on an org chart like legitimate power is. Coercive power is the ability to influence someone through threats, punishment, or intimidation. It's essentially using fear to get someone to do what you want. Bosses might use coercive power in tandem with their legitimate power. For example, a manager might threaten to fire an employee if they don't meet an unrealistic deadline or quota. I can still recall one day at my high school job, working at a movie theater, when I overheard our regional director tell my boss, the theater manager, that if one of my coworkers made another mistake at the cash register to "just fire her ass because at the end of the day your numbers damn well better match."

As disturbing as that sounds, it was a combination of legitimate power and coercive power. The regional director was forcing the theater manager to do the dirty work, while also using the threat of firing someone over their mistakes. Outside of the hierarchy, coercive power can still be used as a weapon. A colleague might also use guilt or threats to get you to agree to do something you don't want to do. Coercive power is a pretty negative way to go about getting what you want. It might get short-term results, but it breeds resentment and harms overall satisfaction in business and relationships.

Expert Power

Expert power is derived from possessing skills or knowledge in a particular area. It's about being recognized due to your expertise, leading to some level of influence and respect from others. An example we've probably all experienced is the high regard we have for our computer and IT experts at work. No matter what their title or position on the org chart, we can't really function without the wonderful work of our nearby tech guru, even if they are just reminding us to reboot our computer or unplug and replug our printer. When it comes to expert power, I might include Mandy in this category. She really was creative. She knew how to come up with the ideas that were treasured by our sales reps and left our clients in awe. She had the expertise to help our sales team close deals and that made her quite powerful in my TechFirm department, even if her brilliant ideas were often far from realistic.

But there's another side to this. Let's step back for a moment and let a version of your future self (me) share another revelation with you. The very reason I was hired at TechFirm is because of my brick-and-mortar shopping mall experience. Expertise. Even on day one, I had a level of expert power nobody could deny and nobody else could claim. Expert power comes from skills and knowledge, not just a job title. I should have known this. My hiring manager Jim knew this and actually made that clear to me when he was telling me how to sell myself to our HR department. At the time, I just didn't realize it. I had expert power but I was too quick to give it up, to defer to others. This is something to keep in mind. You do have a level of expertise, that's why you were hired in the first place.

Informational Power

Informational power is related to expert power in that it refers to the influence you wield by controlling, sharing, or withholding valuable information. This kind of power allows the user the ability to affect others' decisions and actions through information they have access to, exclusive or sought-after knowledge. You have informational power. In fact, your informational power might be another reason why you were hired. Like with expert power, you were hired to do something important enough to be paid for it. Go ahead and repeat that line to yourself. You were hired to do something important enough that they would pay you to do it.

Connection Power

Connection power is the control and the influence you enjoy through your network of relationships. It's the idea that "who you know" can open doors and create opportunities that might not be available otherwise. With connection power, you control your Rolodex, to use an old-fashioned office supply store term for the people you know and can reach out to. Connection power can be vital if your job is in sales, because you know the right people to call in order to set up a meeting or build a relationship. Connection power can also be vital in terms of finding the right consultants and people to hire. Mandy's connection to Ronnie, my boss's boss, might have been her greatest power of all. In fact, it was my connection power that helped me get my job at TechFirm in the first place!

When I knew I had to escape my shopping mall job, I spent a lot of time scouring the want ads (again, late 1980s technology at work here). When I saw the ad for TechFirm, I reached out to two former Ohio State classmates I knew were already working there. And honestly, the two I reached out to were a couple of guys I knew from our shared classes, but I would not have called them close friends. But they came through for me. They were both in a different department, so I can't blame them for the situation I walked into, or if they even knew what was going on with Jim, Mandy, and Ronnie. Early in your career, you might not have a lot of strong connections but you do have connections. You have classmates, you have family, you have teachers. My connections to my OSU classmates weren't strong, but they were strong enough to get the job done.

Reward Power

This type of power is straightforward: who controls the rewards? Reward power can be related to legitimate power and coercive power in that one person, often higher up on the organizational chart, has access to or can control something another person desires. In the business context, rewards include salary increases and promotions, of course. Other kinds of rewards you might not think of at first can include being assigned to desirable, high-exposure projects, and even being protected from less-desirable assignments or committees. Reward power is another kind of control you will not have in your hands early in your career. From my Eastland experience, I had no kind of rewards to offer Lena. I sure couldn't offer her less work than the total absence of work that she was already (not) doing for me. At TechFirm, again, I had nothing to offer anybody but my hard work and creativity. Looking back, I suppose I could have saved my best ideas for my favorite sales reps or my favorite clients. Just writing that idea out makes me uncomfortable with that sort of passive-aggressive behavior. I would never recommend anything more than total effort. So with no rewards to hand out, you might feel powerless and out of control Once again, though, consider the overlaps. You may not be able to hand out raises or promotions, but you will have information and expertise at your disposal.

Referent Power

Referent power might actually have been the biggest difference between Mandy and me. This kind of power refers to the influence you have based on the charisma you demonstrate, the respect and admiration you inspire. Our clients wanted bold ideas and our sales reps wanted to close their deals. Mandy was the one who made it happen. Referent power here is based more on what we might call soft skills than your title or pay grade. The people you work with, including colleagues, clients, and even your bosses, are more likely to listen to and follow ideas of someone they admire or respect, even if those ideas don't come from above. The skills that lead to referent power are skills you might have early in your career. Your personality might be what helped you get hired. You can also build relationships based on your authenticity, your trustworthiness, and your energy. I can still remember early in my current job at Dominican University that my Dean offered me an important departmental project (which included a conference trip to Florida) because, in his words, "even though you're new here, people trust you."

Doing it All Over Again

With these different kinds of power, or control, in mind, let's revisit and learn from the past. When it comes to Lena, Mandy, and Chet, what could I have done? What kind of power did I have over this situation even though I did not realize it back then? We always underestimate how much power we have. In the case of my difficulties with my non-secretary, Lena, it's true I had some legitimate power. But not much. Formally speaking, she worked for my boss, not me. Coercive power? That wasn't my style then – or ever, for that matter. In a situation like this, informational power and expert power can be useful, but only if those you are trying to persuade have any interest in your information or expertise. Connection power? Not at that stage of my career. How about reward power? Like legitimate power, that was in my boss Whit's bag of tricks, not mine. I really didn't have anything to offer Lena at this point.

Chapter 1: I Feel Like I Have No Control

With Lena, it had to come down to referent power. If I were in something like a Lena situation today, where I wanted or needed a colleague to take on more (or any) responsibility, I'd ask her to join me for a coffee or lunch meeting to talk about the situation in a fairly neutral place. There, I would simply explain what happened in an effort to clear the air. No blaming. No gaslighting. I would admit I needed to be more clear in my communications in the future and I will be going forward. Most importantly, I would try to build or rebuild our relationship. Here, in my first job with my first secretary, I had just taken our relationship for granted. Mostly, I needed to establish trust. Since there was no food court or coffee shops in our mall, we would have had to settle for lunch at the hot dog stand at the entrance to Woolworth's, just a few steps away from the office. Thankfully, there are more coffee shops around now than there were in the late 1980s so you can't use that as an excuse in your own life!

In the case of Mandy the challenge would have been greater. Due to her success with our clients, our sales reps, and her best friend relationship with my Director, Ronnie, you might say Mandy held all the cards and all the power. Mandy's style reminded me more of a hit-and-run kind of approach, coming up with big ideas and then running away to the next meeting and leaving me and our support team to bring her ideas into reality. Or to clean up her mess. But now, with the passage of time, I can see how similar Mandy's style was to that of Pablo, my freewheeling mall regional manager. Did you notice this too? So, does that mean my relationship with Mandy was like my boss Whit's relationship with Pablo?

In this scenario, Mandy was like Pablo, filled with great ideas without a lot of concern about how far from reality they might be. The logical next step in this thought process would be that I was like my boss Whit, and as odd as that might seem, it makes sense in dealing with Mandy. While my patron Jim, the guy who hired me at TechFirm, was out of the picture pretty early on, the reason he hired me was my shopping mall experience and that was still in play. Looking back, I might have leaned more into the expertise I already had in terms of idea execution more than idea creation. It would have been a disservice to try to squelch Mandy's ideas and her creativity, but I could have worked with her and my sales reps, using my expertise proactively, to create systems or processes that would help me and our account support teams make Mandy's big promises happen.

Finally, what could I have done about Chet and the situation I found myself in at Chicagoland? In the academic world, a department chair would not be a professor's boss in the same way Whit and Pablo were my Eastland Mall bosses or Ted and Ronnie were my TechFirm bosses. Chet still had power though. The chair still controls important scheduling, project, and budgetary resources for the department. Reward power. To a new kid on the block like me, Chet had even more control, power I bestowed upon him, even if the org chart didn't say the same. The best way to deal with Chet might have been to do more research and publishing and get tenure. But that's what we in the business call "counterfactual thinking," devising some kind of alternate reality. True, the last few paragraphs have been filled with counterfactual thinking and other kinds of "what ifs" and "if onlys."

To say I just should have been better at something I simply was not doesn't do any of us any good. I did have a resource though and therefore some level of control. I spent the six years before Chicagoland as a grad student at the University of Michigan. There, I worked closely for years with my dissertation chair and committee, not to mention the many business professors and other faculty who were part of my training. This includes the junior faculty at Michigan whom I witnessed going through many of the same pressures, stressors, and uncertainties I was now facing. Where were all these connections when I needed them the most? They were right there. I should have called. Maybe they weren't waiting by the phone or checking their email daily waiting for me to reach out. That's not on them. They were still there, doing their work, living their lives, vast resources of information and experience I never tapped into. Like I said, we always underestimate how much power we have. What good is power if you don't know what to do with it or how to use it?

Chapter 2: Nobody Listens to Me

At my first job at Eastland Mall, when I was hired I felt nervous. This was my first real full time job. Growing up with a stay-at-home mom and a dad who owned his own auto parts store and then moved to selling cars for a living left me ignorant about and unexposed to the life and expectations of a suit-wearing careerist. You already saw how awkwardly I handled my regional manager Pablo's request to spray paint many acres of grass green in order to overcome the edicts of nature when it's November and the lawn grows brown. At this, my first full-time job, I felt like a kid in an oversized business suit getting laughed at by the grown ups. Kind of like Tom Hanks in *Big* but without the magical Zoltar fortune telling machine helping me to grow up as fast as I wanted to. But I did feel a lot like Hanks's adult-sized child character, Josh Baskin, when he was confronted with a ridiculous idea: "I don't get it." I just didn't have the guts to say that out loud.

Shortly after that landscaping experience, my manager Whit told me "it's time to haul out the boxes." To provide a little context, Whit and I started each week by taking a Monday morning stroll around the outside and then the inside of our 80-store mall. We would catch up on weekend foot traffic, sales results, and any events that had occurred and then plan our projects for the coming week. As productive as that was, it would be inaccurate to say teaching or mentoring took place during those walks. Not a lot of guidance or teaching. It was pretty much as it sounded, exchanging numbers and plotting out a to-do list. It would also be inaccurate to say that hauling out the boxes was any more than the task it sounded like. With all the excitement and passion of a man describing cardboard boxes (which is pretty much how he described everything), my boss told me to get our U-Haul large moving boxes out of storage and have my information booth staff decorate those boxes with wrapping paper. We would then place these boxes around the mall with some old, bent poster board signs requesting donations for our annual food drive.

"That's it?" I asked.

"That's it. No big deal." With that, Whit walked away back to our office.

I called after him. "Can I do anything with this?" He stopped. "With what?"

Keep in mind that my MBA was less than a year old, the ink on the diploma barely dried, and at this point I had something to prove. "With the food drive… can we make it fun?"

"Well Dave," my boss drawled. "You may do whatever you want. Just don't spend any money on this. It's just a canned food drive."

Wait a minute! Did he sort of just say "Yes"? Did he really hear me? Maybe he even liked this concept of having fun? As tepid as Whit's response was, I was encouraged and embraced this opportunity. And that opportunity, this canned food drive, turned out to be one of the highlights of my one very long year at Eastland Mall. I learned two of my colleagues… assistant mall managers like me at two of the other Columbus malls in Pablo's region, Westland and Northland… received the same orders from their respective bosses. With Whit's orders not to do anything or spend any money on my mind, I called Carrie at Westland and Bob at Northland to see how they were going about their tasks and if they wanted to brainstorm. Bob did not. After all, to him, there was nothing to brainstorm about. Haul out the boxes and put some wrapping paper on them. Bob wanted to become a mall manager himself.

On the other hand, Carrie did not want to become a mall manager. She hated her job as I hated mine, but she did want to share ideas. So Carrie and I put our brains together and came up with a plan. We created an event, starting with those big empty boxes. To summarize our scheme, Carrie and I agreed that while placing non-perishable food items into a box in and of itself might not really sound like a lot of fun, throwing those same cans of food into those same boxes could be more interesting. Maybe a little repressed aggression boiling to the surface for both of us. And from there our conversation evolved from throwing cans of beans and boxes of macaroni and cheese into a cardboard box to shooting a basketball into a hoop. We leaped into action.

At our request, our Sears stores donated basketballs and hoops and backboards… the portable wheeled kind for Carrie's mall, and the kind that could be bolted onto the tall wooden walls surrounding staging areas around some construction taking place inside of my mall. Many of our respective mall stores donated prizes and gift certificates, thrilled to participate in an event that might get a lot of people into the mall and therefore, they hoped, into their post-holiday season stores. Carrie, with her pre-mall public relations experience, staged a joint press conference before the event and convinced one of our local television stations and a radio station to cover what we called

"Hoops for the Hungry" at our two malls. We had something special brewing here. Sorry Bob, you had your chance.

My excitement was off the charts. Carrie and I had built a full-fledged civic event. This was the second most exciting thing to happen to me that week, after the birth of my first child. Yes it's true, my beautiful little boy was just a few days old on the day of this landmark event. Bring him along, I told my wife. I even got a speeding ticket heading to the shopping center. And the mall was a sight to behold. We had television reporters covering our event and our malls ended up on the local evening news. We had radio coverage throughout the day. We had celebrities, like past football players from Ohio State and current basketball players from the school's NCAA tournament-caliber basketball team. That included a young hoopster named Jay Burson, a college star adored in Columbus and throughout Ohio even if, some 35 years later, you don't know his name. This is quite significant since Jay was there, in my mall, wearing a halo traction brace screwed into his skull, the kind of device you wear to immobilize your broken neck since Jay had indeed broken his neck two months earlier in a basketball game against Iowa. Jay was in my mall! He even signed my Hoops for the Hungry poster!

At Eastland we ended up with people lined up inside our mall - twice around! - waiting for the opportunity to exchange their food for a chance to make a free throw and win a prize and meet a local sports celebrity. We set a food donation record, according to our friends at the Central Ohio Food Bank. And beyond the good deed that we did, we gained hundreds of thousands of dollars of publicity (in 1989 dollars), including video footage on the local news, not to mention a ton of goodwill from the community and from our retailers. The retailers, as you might guess, really liked having hundreds of new happy customers in the mall, checking out their stores. And you know who else was happy? Our maintenance and security teams. I had taken it upon myself to add a couple of guys to handle the crowd that day, and in addition to some overtime pay, the two crews had a blast playing a little ongoing pick-up game for a few minutes every hour or so during our brief breaks. This April event, starting with no more than a bunch of beat up cardboard boxes was an incredible success for both of our shopping malls.

Two days later, on that next Monday, the mall looked to be back to normal and I couldn't wait to check in on our merchants to see their reactions. Whit and I took our weekly walk around the mall and I asked him if he had even made it to our event or if he saw it on the news. Amidst all of the activity and noise and hundreds of guests and shoppers in our mall, I had not seen him anywhere. He said he was there but for just a little while. "What did you think?" I asked him, like a puppy in need of praise. I quote his response, burned into my memory:

"Do you have any idea how much overtime we had to pay for security and maintenance? Next time, just stick with the boxes." And then Whit walked back to his office.

I had never felt so unseen, so unheard, or like such a poor fit in my environment. All that hard work, that collaboration, that creativity. All those people at the event, all the local celebrities, all that publicity! And that speeding ticket, as I raced with my wife and newborn son to get to this big event, the biggest project of my life up to that point… just waved away, dismissed.

Of course I wondered what I did wrong. Is this happening because I was still the new kid on the block? Because I was still only 24 years old, too young to be trusted to make grown-up decisions? Because Whit resented anything creative, anything that seemed to have any hint of Pablo's fingerprints on it? All I know is that I did my best, got objectively positive results, and was still shut down and rejected by my boss. Does that sound at all familiar to you?

And to be clear, this was not one of those "ask forgiveness, not permission" scenarios gone wrong. This event did not catch my boss by surprise, and he had even admired how little money I had spent in the weeks leading up to the event… basically, none. But lamenting over the overtime wages we had to pay to make Hoops for the Hungry happen was his only response. Over a three-month time-frame, with Carrie's help, I had tried to assert some measure of control over my work environment. Yet just when I wanted to celebrate what I had achieved through my efforts on this project over the preceding months, my boss stripped that power right away.

Ceding Control

Something I'm discovering even as I write this, and I hope you are discovering as you read this: we have control and at least some measure of power, even when we start a new job or a new chapter of our careers. But it's easy to let that control slip away. Or to have it taken away. For example, when I left Eastland to go to TechFirm, I was hand-picked by Jim, the creator of our Electronic Shopper, but was soon overwhelmed by our creative consultant Mandy. At my first academic job at Chicagoland, I thought my first day was my worst day, but somehow it still went downhill from there. I was misguided and mismentored until I was finally and figuratively escorted out the door. In all three of my early jobs, I had some measure of control, power as we defined in Chapter 1. Now why in the world would someone cede control, give power away? Or allow it to be taken? It's not that simple but I can think of a few reasons. These reasons include comparison, overwhelm, lack of awareness, and, especially, self-doubt.

Comparison: When we start a new job or in a new environment, we immediately stand out simply because we're the new kid on the block. It's also possible we are younger than our new colleagues, or even older. Others at work will wonder about us, why we were hired (if they weren't involved in the process… or even if they were!), what we will contribute, what talents we bring to the table… even how much we're being paid. The comparisons are inevitable. Given our newness, we might surrender a level of power or control because we think someone else deserves it more than we do or someone else can use it better than we can. That is, we might cede control due to feelings of inadequacy compared to others. This reminds me of the situation I walked into at Chicagoland.

Overwhelm: This seems more likely when we're younger than when we're a little more experienced, but any time you step into a new environment, it can be like the firehose was turned on, aimed right between your eyes. We might be overwhelmed by the sheer amount of information dropped onto our laps. We might also be awed or overwhelmed by somebody else's authority or power. We might feel run over. I immediately think of Mandy at TechFirm in this case. I was transitioning from Eastland, with just a few of us in charge and one simple model of organizational structure and hierarchy to TechFirm, a cubicle farm with room-sized computers and thousands of employees and dozens of departments. TechFirm was a toolbox filled with equipment I was unfamiliar with. And speaking of overwhelm, don't forget Mandy. Her personality was forceful and her presence felt constant even if she was back in New York. And she had the support not only of her good friend, my boss's boss, but also of the sales reps to whom she was so helpful. The fact that my account support reps and I resented her involvement was meaningless. The state of feeling overwhelmed can lead you to having power taken away, or simply dropped while concentrating on other activities.

Lack of Awareness: The reasons for ceding power in this category can be summarized not realizing we even have any control or authority. These reasons suggest we might not be aware of the power we hold or the potential benefits of using it. I feel like this might have been my case with Lena back at Eastland. After she decided she didn't work for me anymore, I can imagine myself passively wondering if she ever really worked for me at all. That's not something I'm proud of, along with how the whole debacle played out over my last months at Eastland. Now on the other end of the spectrum, I can also remember the time, late in my stay at TechFirm where the mall group brought in a new employee. My boss at that time, Arnold, introduced me to Prue and let me know she would be there to help me with my projects, help me with whatever I needed. At that time, I simply didn't understand. Oh, is Prue my assistant? I thought I was doing just fine. That was then, anyway. Today, I realize that's how I might have misinterpreted that situation. I didn't realize what kind of meaningful leadership opportunity was presented to me.

Self-Doubt: We might cede control simply because we don't think we deserve it, we think we're not ready, and we might even think we won't understand what to do with the power we have. Power, authority, control over our situations, even our careers, can be scary if we think we're not ready for it. These all point to a lack of confidence or feeling unprepared for the responsibility that comes with control. There can also be more external generators of our self-doubt. This category would include reasons like somebody telling us we don't deserve any control or power, that we haven't earned it, and that we even should not really have any such influence. These reasons all point to forces influencing or manipulating us into giving up control.

Imposter Syndrome

At this point, I want to say a few words about something related to self-doubt called "Imposter syndrome." Imposter syndrome is all over the place, maybe now more than ever. I first heard the term early in my doctoral student career, sometime during the early 1990s. And I hear it today, among even my finest students. The concept of imposter syndrome, originally called "imposter phenomenon" was first brought forth in 1978. This term had been around for 15 years or so when I first learned about the concept, but it's still a fairly recent idea or at least a fairly new name for a longer-standing idea. Am I an imposter? No. Maybe sometimes. I don't know. Are you?

Actually, here's my answer: No, I'm not an imposter even if my self-confidence wavers every now and then. If I may own my origin story, my truth: I've got a PhD. I've got an MBA. I've been deemed capable and qualified enough to teach people marketing in college, graduate school, and executive education. I've got a big piece of paper in my house that says so. Then again, a few years back a cable repairman was in my house, in my home office where that big piece of paper hangs on a wall surrounded by a thick frame, and surrounded by other framed diplomas, mine and my wife's. After the cable guy solved what was probably some easily repaired technical issue, I exclaimed "Wow! That's it?" In response, he muttered "I guess there's all kinds of smart in the world." First of all, I heard that, mister. Second of all, ouch. I'm not paying you money to hurt my feelings. If that's what he was even trying to do. And here I am years later still talking about it.

David Aron

Imposter syndrome is real and it's something experienced by a great many people. Dr. Amy Cuddy, who has taught at Harvard, Northwestern, and a couple of other places you might have heard of that also didn't hire me during my 1998 job search (described later in this chapter), defines imposter syndrome as *"a collection of feelings of inadequacy that persist despite evident success."* Dr. Cuddy adds that up to 80% of people feel like they're frauds at one point in their life. That number might be even higher, based on some recent conversations I've had with students who readily admit they feel like imposters, and a great many students and colleagues who might acknowledge their own feelings but less directly.

As an aside to my original aside, one of the most important things you can do for yourself is recognize the skills and talents that you possess. Know the lessons you've learned and the powers you've earned are rightfully yours. In a few minutes I'll go into more detail about the importance of identifying and honoring your origin story and we'll talk about your strengths and what I call your Superpower Portfolio in the next chapter. But for now, yes, cable guy, I'm grateful you understood how to solve my entertainment problem in a way I could not.

Imposter syndrome is complicated. Really complicated. You might feel like an imposter whether you are young or old, male or female, skilled or unskilled, regarded as a high achiever by others or not. It might happen because you are always struggling in comparison to those around you. Even if you really aren't. And this is in no way meant to minimize your struggles or those of the people around you. We don't know what's going on inside someone else's mind, yet our interpretations of this unknown might cause stress to ourselves. There can be a surprising gulf between perception and reality. And believe me, social media does not help. Maybe you've heard this before but it's worth repeating: on whichever social media you're using, you are seeing someone else's chosen, hand-selected presentation of themself, their highlights, their best self. You are reading about people bragging about their latest achievement while you are in the middle of your typical day. Why would anybody listen to you when your social media platform pals have such amazing things going on in their lives?

On the other hand, imposter syndrome might occur because everything has always come easily for you and everybody compliments you on how smart or talented you are. Yeah, you're lucky. Your success comes from outside of you. But what about all the hard work you've done to put yourself in the position to be so lucky, to take advantage of the opportunities that have presented themselves to you? What about your origin story, all you've been through to get to where you are? Let me return to my exchange with the cable guy. When I cried out "Wow! That's it?" after he fixed my television problem, his first thought might have been "yeah, all it took was attaching this cable to that outlet. That and many years of training and experience and crawling around other people's houses. I just make it look easy." That could be what led to his muttered reply.

The seminal work on imposter syndrome involved the study of high achieving women, objectively talented and capable people who still didn't feel like they deserved what they were achieving. That feeling might have been external, coming from the outside, or internal, from the inside, or even a combination, lowered self-esteem coming from a worn down inside after a lifetime of pressure from the outside. Even I can be self-deprecating to the point of annoying those around me. A colleague once told me, after I made a self-inflicted insult, that "it's not as cute as you think it is." Ouch again. I wasn't even trying to be cute. And you know what? She was right. **Don't put yourself down.** And don't bother circling that sentence or dog-earing this page. Just remember it. Say it out loud. Starting now, don't put yourself down. It's not cute.

The point here is to tell you that you are not an imposter. You don't need to fake it til you make it. You don't need to fake it at all. You might have to take the slow train up the learning curve, especially if you are new to your job or industry or career. But don't fake anything. After all, to make sure you are not an imposter, hiring firms and admitting schools will put in the work, look at your grades, interview you, and ask for letters of reference to make sure you are who they need you to be. In my search for my first academic position (two years before I was hired at Chicagoland), I went through a grueling job hunt. Part of this process included letters of reference, sent from my professors and advisors to the schools searching for a new marketing professor, just to make sure I was who I was supposed to be.

See What Others See

And that brings us to my advisor, mentor, and dissertation chair at Michigan, a man named Rick. At the risk of being too over the top, Rick was amazing. The best. Rick recently retired and I'm referring to my relationship with him from over 25 years ago. He was a gifted, gentle teacher. He was an amazing scholar and researcher. His work was seminal, transcendent, all the words we use to describe brilliance. I was so lucky he let me work with him. At the time of his retirement, he held three different professorial positions at one of the elite universities in the world. And that just scratches the surface.

Rick wrote a letter of reference on my behalf as part of the job search process, as dissertation chairs do for their students. Of course I waived my right to see the letter and yet somehow I ended up with a copy. I don't think it was supposed to be hidden in the pile of papers and articles he handed to me that one day but there it was, and of course I read it. Wouldn't you? Well, I recognized the name at the top… it was spelled just like mine… but the rest of the letter? That doesn't look like me at all. Exactly who is Rick writing about here? This "Dave" person is amazing! While he is just starting his new career, Dave is earning his PhD from a great school, his teaching skills are top-notch, and his research is fresh, creative, and has far-reaching implications. Wow, Rick seemed to see something special in me.

Letters of reference or phone calls for the same purpose are a typical part of every job search, but for future faculty members, the process becomes a little bit different than what most job seekers in other industries encounter. After those letters are sent out by dissertation chairs around the world on behalf of their students, a key event in the job searches of many grad students is something called a "jobs conference." This is a gathering of professors and researchers where, like at most conferences, research findings are shared, ideas are discussed, and connections are made. Meanwhile, out of sight of the rest of the conference attendees, the hallways of the host hotel or facility are swarmed by graduate students, bouncing from room to room to interview with representatives of schools looking to hire people just like me or, more likely, this Dave that Rick wrote about. And the best thing about that Dave is that he seems to be nothing less than a young version of his dissertation chair, Rick. And Rick is among the most highly respected and beloved members of his field.

Before the jobs conference, letters like the one Rick wrote for me are sent out by dissertation chairs to the schools their grad students hope to work at. Because I was still fairly young and very naive, and I probably had not checked first with my wife, I gave Rick a very long list of schools at which I would love to work, many based on his recommendations. Now here's a key point: the schools Rick wrote to are some pretty amazing schools: Harvard, Princeton, Yale, Northwestern, University of Chicago, Pepperdine, University of North Carolina, and more. In all, I ended up with 17 interviews over the several days I would spend at that year's jobs conference. This was in large part because of Rick's reputation and the fact that I was his student. Perhaps his protégé. And yet as I began to roam the halls I felt like a very scared little kid in a very big candy store. Like that kid in the movie *Big* all over again.

Making a Name for Yourself

I have a couple stories that summarize the whole jobs conference experience. The first is from my interview with Harvard University on the very first day of the conference. Harvard! What a way to start! I was in a hotel room with two marketing professors whom I had already heard of, each with enormous stature in my field. The conversation seemed to go well, although I might have spent too much time staring at the Mickey Mouse tie one of my interviewers was wearing. As our interview concluded, the more senior of the two (with that Disney tie) excused himself for a moment and stepped into another room in the suite. A moment later, when he returned, he was licking the back of a thin envelope, which he pressed closed and handed to me. He grinned. "Here, Dave," he said. "We absolutely will not hire you. There's just no way, not now, not ever. After we read that letter of recommendation, we thought we might be getting a younger version of Rick and young man, that is not you. I just thought the merciful thing to do would be to tell you now so you wouldn't have to wait to find out."

Chapter 2: Nobody Listens to Me

Other than the whimsical tie and the part about not getting hired, the rest of that story didn't really happen quite that way. Professor Mickey Mouse did not really hand me my rejection letter then and there. It actually took two whole days for the letter to arrive, and for me to find out they would not hire me, not now, not ever. The letter got to my house before the conference was even over, that's how quickly they made their decision not to hire me. But here is another story that really did happen. I won't name this school because of my relationships with people who work there now. Let's go back to the next day of the jobs conference when I interviewed with another couple of professors from this school on the opposite coast. This time, the senior interviewer asked his junior to go to the other room and get all of us cups of coffee. This seemed weird so late in the meeting and it made me get all excited. Is that how these things work when I'm acing the interview? Extended private conversation with the guy in charge! Was I about to get an offer? Are we going to talk about salary? Then, the interviewer spoke to me.

"Dave, how are you feeling?"

"Great!"

"Dave, as I'm sure you know, our university is rooted in our Church of Christ heritage. Are you a member of the Church of Christ?"

"Uh, no, I am not."

"That's okay, Dave. Many members of our community are Christian but wouldn't identify as members of the Church of Christ."

I nodded along. "Okay."

"Dave, are you an active member of your church?"

My nodding slowed down. "I really am not."

"Are you Muslim? Many of our...."

"No, I'm not."

"Oh. Okay." He looked down and shuffled his papers.

A pause, and then I spoke. "I guess we're done, aren't we?"

He didn't look up. "No... not necessarily." He said, as his partner returned with our coffee.

I did not drink my coffee. I said, "Thank you," politely excused myself, and left.

It wasn't all weird and bad, though. From those 17 interviews, I did get exactly one second interview and a subsequent job offer. Thank you, Northeastern. However, my wife and I were still a couple of Great Lakes midwestern kids with three small children of our own and we just were not ready for Boston at that time.

Back to imposter syndrome. My job search experience revealed to me that something was wrong with me. I was not worth hiring. Sixteen of the best schools in the USA told me I was not who they thought I was, confirming to me (at that time) that I was not who I was expected to be, who I was supposed to be. So yeah, I've felt like an imposter.

As prevalent and staggering as imposter syndrome is for so many people, it's not the only experience that can make you feel like you don't belong. Let's compare the job interview gauntlet to my prior experiences. At Ohio State, I didn't feel like an imposter as much as I received a lot of evidence that I might not be ready for Master's-level classwork. At Eastland Mall, I didn't feel like an imposter, I just felt frustrated; I did not have opportunities to demonstrate I did have some talent and ideas. I was always either stuck between my two feuding bosses or stonewalled by my secretary.

At TechFirm, I don't think I felt like an imposter either. By definition, an imposter is someone pretending to be something they're not. The TechFirm situation was more of a case where I didn't really even know who I was or who I was supposed to be. I'd say I was more adrift and unformed, maybe even experiencing an existential crisis, than I was an imposter. Then at Chicagoland, I was still reeling from the job search the year prior. For context, my second job search involved only two schools, and only Chicagoland offered me a job. But then I got there and it seemed like they went and moved the goalposts during the period between the day they hired me and the day I started my job, which even to this day those in my academic world find hard to believe. I wasn't an imposter, just someone hired for a role that no longer existed.

The Cure to the Syndrome

If you feel like you're experiencing Imposter Syndrome, even some of the time, you can look up how to combat this feeling. I'll save you a few minutes of online search time and let you know there are a lot of approaches you might take, including meditation, journaling, stepping away from your desk, even reaching out to a trusted friend or mentor. I've tried them all. They can all work sometimes. To gain a longer-term benefit, beyond the immediate problem or situation in front of you, I recommend this:

Remember how you got to where you are.

David Aron

What is your origin story? Think about it and own it.

Now you might be wondering, when I say "origin story" am I talking about something like baby Superman being put in a rocket ship by his mom and dad, sent to Earth from an exploding planet Krypton?

Yes.

Am I talking about unpopular teenage nerd Peter Parker being bitten by a spider that had been bathed in radiation during an experiment conducted at a high school field trip that turned him into Spider-Man?

Yes to that too.

Am I talking about Tony Stark having no choice but to build an exoskeleton, a metal suit that kept his damaged heart beating while also helping him escape from his captors as Iron Man?

Yes again.

I'm pretty certain none of those things really happened to you, or to anyone outside of some classic comic books and superhero movies. But what if we look at it like this: can you think of anyone who left one environment for a new one and, upon arriving, discovered that they had unique skills and gifts? Maybe you? Or someone who was involved in an unexpected situation that revealed they had talents they didn't realize they had? Maybe you? Or someone who found they were in an uncomfortable or intolerable situation and realized they had no choice but to save themselves and escape? Maybe you?

And definitely me. See if any of these sound familiar:

Chapter 2: Nobody Listens to Me

- After being cast out from Chicagoland, where my research productivity was deemed inadequate by their standards, I arrived at Dominican University where my weakness became my strength. I suddenly became one of the most productive researchers in my department and a mentor to others.

- Before that, toward the end of my stay at TechFirm (although I didn't know this at that time), I was surprised to be asked to create and run an important research project alongside a more experienced marketing research consultant. Through this unexpected event I realized I enjoyed research and was pretty good at it.

- That same project led me to become embroiled in a difficult ethical quandary and the experienced researcher I worked with helped guide me out of that situation, out of professional danger and toward graduate school, leading to my acquiring a whole new set of talents and changing the trajectory of my career forever.

Your origin story isn't just a made-up story about some fictional character's journey. It is YOUR personal journey filled with training, experiences, learning, and earning the right to hold your position where you work and in your community. Take ownership of your narrative and see how it connects to the larger stories around you. Owning your origin story helps you to uncover your own strengths and gifts. Your origin story reminds you of the effort, the hard work it took to get you where you are. Whether you are a cable repairman, a degreed academic, a CEO, CMO, CFO, or one of ten newly hired associates, you have an origin story worth celebrating. Reflecting on your journey, the challenges you've overcome, and the skills you've developed can help you to recognize how your story connects to the larger narrative of your career and your contributions to your community or field. In short, when you own your origin story you recognize your accomplishments and see challenges as part of your journey, not evidence of your inadequacy. You are the hero in your story, not an imposter.

Chapter 3: You Own Your Origin Story

To help you see yourself as the hero of your own story and overcome imposter syndrome, let's spend this chapter focused on crafting your unique origin story. Understanding your strengths and weaknesses is essential not only for your own development but also in identifying the right mentors to guide you along the way, to help you fill in the gaps among your own experiences and superpowers. The ideas I share with you in this chapter will help you build the confidence to recognize your value, define your goals, and grow by stepping out of your comfort zone. Together, we'll explore how to harness your strengths, confront your weaknesses, and ultimately, find the mentors who can help you unlock your full potential. Let's get to work in planning your own career trajectory.

Throughout this book you are reading my origin story. Before we go too much further, let me ask you: What is your origin story? You know you have one. What events, decisions, or challenges have brought you to where you are now? Now, bear with me for a moment: I don't want to completely geek out on superhero stories, but as a kid, I was captivated by the comics. I was a fan and a collector with thousands of issues, valuable old comics and new ones, at least until I quit cold-turkey the day I graduated from high school. And yeah, I'm the guy who sold the collection for pennies on the dollar to pay for grad school. Since that time, the world has caught up on the superhero craze. The Hollywood movie industry has turned superheroes like Spider-Man, Avengers, Superman, Wonder Woman, Batman, and others into billion-dollar businesses and integral parts of our popular culture.

Superheroes are a beloved form of fantasy and entertainment, and they provide us with an exciting template for understanding our own lives. Of course these stories are fictional. Importantly, they can serve as powerful metaphors. As I shared in Chapter 2, none of us are actually Spider-Man or Iron Man. I can say with almost 100% certainty that none of us were sent to Earth in a spaceship before our planet blew up. And yet realistically, our own origin stories may be just as transformative. Because they are real. Could your story include moving out of a toxic situation and discovering new strengths in a new place?

It happened to me. I went from being a good-enough teacher but a struggling researcher in one environment to becoming an innovative, productive researcher and teacher in another. Let's take those old comic book tales, strip away the exploding planets and glowing spiders and gamma rays and think about the real-life challenges we've all faced in our careers. Your origin story, no matter how dramatic or seemingly ordinary, is unique. It's yours. And it's real. And like the superheroes we grew up admiring (and still do), you have your own set of superpowers, shaped by your experiences and your skill set.

Your Hero's Journey

If we are going to use the world of superheroes to build your Superpower Portfolio, let's start by placing you in the context of what is known as the Hero's Journey. This is a widely-used storytelling framework many heroes in literature and movies follow. Do you want some examples? How about Harry Potter? Luke Skywalker from the Star Wars movies? Frodo Baggins from the Lord of the Rings stories? We can also include other well-known characters like Simba from The Lion King and Dorothy from The Wizard of Oz. Back in the world of comic books the Hero's Journey pretty much includes all the superheroes. Recent examples include the Black Panther, and Miles Morales, the latter-day Spider-Man from the Spider-Verse movies.

The Hero's Journey is not just about a character's actions, but a deeper process that reflects overcoming obstacles, enjoying personal growth, and experiencing a transformation. This journey, attributed to the late author, Joseph Campbell, includes the similar stages heroes go through, across different cultures and different eras. Let's consider how the Hero's Journey can demonstrate how you too can evolve from an ordinary individual to the hero of your story just like Luke, Simba, Dorothy, and Miles.

The Hero's Journey has been explained in many different forms but we can start with four essential steps: The Call to Adventure, the Supreme Ordeal, the Transformation, and the Road Back Home.

1. Call to Adventure

The first essential step in the Hero's Journey is the Call to Adventure, where your life is disrupted to the extent that your journey begins. The call to adventure can be seen in three steps, starting with your life in your **ordinary world**, the place you are used to. Are you living in that world right now? Think of Peter Parker as the bullied high school student or Harry Potter as the tormented youngster stuck in a tiny room under his relatives' stairs. In my own story, I was aimlessly stumbling around in Columbus, Ohio, working at a job that had little meaning or clarity to me. I was asked to take on a research project for my firm, but this project soon became darkened by an ethical conflict that ran against my own moral compass. I could have remained passive and violated my own code, or taken action for what I thought was right. This conflict was my **call to adventure**. However, my hesitation to leave my comfort zone and move my family was my own version of **refuse the call**, to use the language of the Hero's Journey. Eventually, persuaded by my research project partner, I realized passively refusing this call was never an option for me.

2. Supreme Ordeal or Initiation

Since you could not refuse the call, your Hero's Journey continues to the second essential step, your Supreme Ordeal or your Initiation. When, after leaving TechFirm and corporate life entirely, I think of my years as a doctoral student at the University of Michigan, the term supreme ordeal seems very fitting indeed. And earning my degree was nothing if not an **initiation** into a world I never dreamed of. This was a situation filled with more than one **mentor figure** to offer guidance and companionship. Here, I'm thinking first of my research supervisor, a newly-minted PhD who was just a year older than me but had already earned his doctorate. In the sense that we were both in new environments, he might also be described as a sidekick. Or maybe I was the sidekick for his Hero's Journey! Rick, my dissertation chair, certainly fit the description of a mentor to me.

The next step of the ordeal is called **cross the threshold**, where the hero realizes there is no turning back from their adventure. The ordeal continues a series of tests, involving both allies and enemies. Just a big fat checkmark here, as you'll see that at Michigan, and throughout my entire career journey, I have faced many tests, a few enemies, and some valuable allies. I'm sure you can think of more than a few tests along the way on your own Hero's Journey.

3. Transformation or Unification

Using my own journey as an example, I would define my finishing grad school at Michigan as my transformation, as my unification with the world of college professors. This involved the sub-steps known as the **approach**, or preparing for a major challenge in the journey such as teaching my first class and, of course, my dissertation. The next step is called the **ordeal**, in which the hero's greatest fears may be exposed, but from the ordeal comes a new life for the hero. The **reward** for surviving the ordeal is therefore earned by the hero, transforming from their old life to their new one. But the Hero's Journey is not yet finished.

4. Road Back Home or Hero's Return

To complete the journey, the hero chooses to take the **road back**, to return from where they started, figuratively or literally. In my example, this step would be to return to my life of marketing but with my reward of experiencing a **resurrection**, now as a professor, no longer a lost marketing practitioner. To add another, more literal dimension to this chapter in my journey, in my case I was also able to return to Chicago, where I had lived throughout my whole life, up until 12 years earlier. And, importantly, I brought with me the **magical elixir** of marketing knowledge that I could now share with my students and colleagues. Yet my return to Chicago and my new job were filled with more turmoil that made it difficult for me to embrace my new identity. This led to what can only be called another journey, but one much shorter in length, where I left one school, spent a year at a second institution, and then finally landed at a third school, where I have stayed for nearly 20 years.

This chapter of my story might also be known as **atonement**, having a better understanding of the challenges and responsibilities of my role. In this part of the journey the hero is tested one last time, with the real possibility of having the hero's previous achievements destroyed. And I must admit, during my turmoil while at Chicagoland, I wondered many times if I would survive my journey, at least professionally speaking. On more than one occasion I wondered if I was even meant to be a college professor. If the hero manages to survive these last challenges, they can establish their new home and new, better version of normal.

How about you? Can you think of your own version of the Hero's Journey? Have you started it yet? Or maybe you find yourself in the middle of your quest. Have you had your Call to Adventure? Have you already successfully taken such a journey? Or is the Hero's Journey exactly the kind of adventure you need right now to take control of your career? With this in mind, and to give some personal context to the superpower questions that come next, can you recall your own version of the Adventure, of your Supreme Ordeal or Initiation, of your Unification or Transformation, and of your Road Back home?

Appreciating Your Origin

You might acquire your superpowers during your (super)Hero's Journey, or you might have already had these powers all along. And despite the obvious influence comics have had on my writing (and teaching, and research, and office decorating decisions), I know you probably didn't find a magical Green Lantern Power Ring or get a super soldier serum treatment like Captain America. But it's fun to take those crazy origin stories and think of real world counterparts.

Chapter 3: You Own Your Origin Story

For example, are you like a member of the Fantastic Four, taking a risk, facing failure, and in the process discovering new capabilities you never dreamed of? Maybe you are like one of the X-Men, capable of extraordinary things but needing the right mentor to help you discover your talents. Or the Hulk, stepping out of a place of relative safety and gaining great powers because of it? Could your origin story include moving out of a destructive situation and discovering new powers in your new place? Could something that happened to you accidentally, unexpectedly, lead you to discover the ability to do things you never imagined doing before? Could you have come up with an idea, with your back against the wall, that saved a client or brought on greater responsibility?

My own origin might be like Shazam, finding myself in a strange and unexpected place (Ann Arbor, Michigan), gaining powers from a group of wise and powerful figures. Or maybe more like Doctor Strange, deprived of my abilities and wandering across the Earth (or from central Ohio and into Michigan, in my case), hoping for salvation and in the process gaining a whole new set of gifts. Imagine your origin story, like the heroes you admire, is filled with moments of transformation.

This list takes some of the typical comic book origin stories and translates them into the real world. Please read through these and think about if any of them apply to you… or as more than one of my advisees have told me, if almost all of them do!

1. Discovered a power you didn't know you had

You might have stumbled upon strengths when you were pushed to the limit. These moments may feel ordinary until you realize how much growth they represent.

2. Had something important taken away

Like Doctor Strange losing the use of his hands, you might have experienced the loss of a job or role you once identified with. Yet, in that loss, you discovered a new direction or strength.

3. Lost something important through your own action or inaction

Sometimes, like Peter Parker's legendary story of failing to stop the fleeing robber who eventually shot Peter's beloved uncle, we make mistakes that cost us something important. This loss can become the catalyst for growth, teaching us resilience and the value of accountability.

4. Were forced away from home

Like Superman being sent from his dying home planet, you may have had to leave a familiar environment, only to find that in the discomfort, you developed new skills or found a community that appreciated your talents.

5. Experienced a fateful accident

A seemingly random event in your life might have given rise to skills you never anticipated. This could be an accident or surprise that forced you to adapt in ways that expanded your potential.

6. Chose to or were forced to break the rules

As Wolverine might agree, sometimes rules must be bent or broken to discover new ways of thinking. Just like heroes who operate outside the norm, you may have found your unique approach by stepping out of the usual confines of your industry or community.

7. Had to make a sacrifice

Chapter 3: You Own Your Origin Story

Like so many superheroes, you might have had to give up something important—time, a relationship, or a safe opportunity—only to find the sacrifice led to something even greater.

8. Had to defend something or someone

Whether defending a client, a colleague, or a belief, these moments often reveal your capacity for leadership. Like Captain America standing for his principles, you may find your stance uncovers hidden strengths.

9. Made a discovery, found something that nobody else knew about

Your story may include a moment of revelation, where, like Iron Man building his first suit of armor to escape certain doom, you found a solution or a new path no one else had seen.

10. Had your back against the wall

When the pressure is on, and everything seems against you, this is where many superheroes find their true abilities. Like any hero in a tight spot, you might have discovered you could solve problems under immense pressure.

11. Volunteered or participated in a new activity

Much like how heroes often start as regular people stepping up, you might have discovered a new ability simply by saying "yes" to something unfamiliar, like a leadership role or an unfamiliar task.

12. Sought one thing but discovered another

Doctor Strange was searching for the knowledge to save his surgical career, but found the real reward was something quite different. Maybe you pursued a certain goal only to discover new skills or insights along the way.

13. Sought forgiveness

Seeking redemption, like Thor after being banished from his home in Asgard, is a powerful origin story. Sometimes our growth comes from acknowledging our mistakes and seeking to make amends, gaining humility and perspective in the process.

14. Were taken under someone's guidance

Like Professor X mentoring the X-Men, perhaps a mentor saw something in you before you recognized it yourself. Through their guidance, you were able to see your own potential and grow beyond your limitations.

15. Were called upon to teach someone

Sometimes, teaching others reveals your own strengths. As Spider-Man mentors the younger Miles Morales, you might have found teaching someone else led to deeper insights about your own abilities.

16. Were chosen for a new task or responsibility

Once again, this seems to apply to just about any superhero you can think of. Have you been thrust into a new role that stretched your abilities, revealing strengths you didn't know you had?

17. Sought, were guided by, those with wisdom

Shazam was just a troubled boy who stumbled upon mentors that unlocked a new heroic path for him, leading to his transformation. Have you experienced this as well?

18. Created something unique

Like Tony Stark building Iron Man "in a cave, from a box of scraps" as they say in the movie, maybe you invented, designed, or built something only you could have created. This is your personal stamp on the world, a manifestation of your unique capabilities.

19. Moved to a new environment

Relocating, whether by your choice or by someone else's, can sometimes reveal our ability to adapt and thrive. In a new city or workplace, you might have discovered fresh strengths.

20. Overcame a setback

Like Deadpool surviving a horrible experiment on his body, you may have faced failure or disappointment, only to come back stronger and more resilient.

21. Were exposed to something new or strange

New experiences can be disorienting, but they often help us grow. Perhaps you found yourself in an unfamiliar situation and, like Guardians of the Galaxy, learned to navigate a strange new world.

22. Faced failure

The Fantastic Four's comic book miscalculations led them to gain their superpowers, and your missteps may end up leading you to surprisingly strong outcomes. Failure can be your best teacher. In your story, these moments of failure often reveal the grit and determination that define your character.

23. Learned of your strengths from a boss, coach, mentor

Sometimes we can't see our strengths until someone else points them out. Like a coach seeing an athlete's potential, a mentor or teacher may have been the one to reveal your hidden talents. As you'll see, I credit my research partner from TechFirm for noticing I had a knack for marketing research that would lead to my career change.

24. Stepped out of a place of relative safety

The comic book version of Bruce Banner left a safe bunker to save a teenager's life. This led to Banner absorbing the gamma radiation that turned him into the Hulk. You too may have had to leave a safe, comfortable situation to gain or discover your real powers.

Just as the superheroes we've looked at uncovered their unique abilities, your Hero's Journey is also defined by pivotal moments that reveal your hidden strengths. Real moments and real strengths, not pretend ones. Whether your powers were born out of risk, failure, or moments of unexpected change, your story is deeply personal and empowering. These are part of your origin story. But what are your superpowers?

Your Superpower Portfolio

If you are going to successfully enjoy your Hero's Journey, you will need strength. This means we must get started on your journey of self-discovery. It's time to pack for the trip. What powers do you possess? What are you good at? What are the talents and skills that set you apart? It's time to take inventory and start building a list of your superpowers. And remember, your origin story isn't just a fantasy—it's real and a reminder of the challenges you've overcome, the people who've helped you along the way, and the responsibility you now have to use your powers wisely. This is about understanding your value, embracing your gifts, and stepping into your talents. Our origins are unique. They are our own. And you are for real. And you have amazing abilities.

Your Origin Story is important for a number of reasons. Think about it. What are your powers and how did you get them? Your origin story is the foundation, and your superpowers are what will propel you forward. Your story illustrates the challenges you've had to overcome. It also reminds you that you have responsibility to those involved, the people who have helped you. Your story is also a reminder that you can "pay it forward" and it helps you understand what "it" is. No matter how you acquired them, you have superpowers. You are not an imposter.

Let's put together your Superpower Portfolio.

First question: What are you good at? Don't be humble. Do any ideas immediately come to mind? Would it help if I provided a little more context? Okay, what are you good at in terms of:

- Your job
- Your hobbies
- When you're with your family
- When you're with your friends
- Even when you're by yourself

Now, there are a couple of ways to examine this question about what you're good at. One approach could simply involve writing down what you know, deep inside, you're good at doing. Maybe you're good at writing or creating videos. Good at public speaking or meeting deadlines or you're good at ice skating, good at baseball, good at crossword puzzles. Even if you don't see any of that directly applying to work... write it down. Even the skills you use outside of work may still indirectly apply to your career. Perhaps you are graceful. Perhaps you have endurance, tenacity, grit... write those things down. This is how we can learn about your superpowers.

There are more ways to build your list. One, like we just said, could be the things you know you're good at in different settings, even if you'll eventually have to sort of translate them from the world of fun to the world of work, to the world of your career. This list can also include what many call "soft skills." This often includes interpersonal, relationship skills that will help you build your network and find success. These include:

- **Problem-Solving:** Your ability to recognize and solve problems is fundamental in almost every job, especially in leadership roles. It's a talent that others are looking for.
- **Active Listening:** This talent is crucial in building strong relationships, fostering collaboration, and resolving conflicts.
- **Empathy:** This means understanding and sharing the feelings of others, which is vital in leadership, teamwork, and customer service.
- **Organizational Skills:** You might be naturally organized and good at managing time or tasks, essential in achieving goals efficiently and reducing stress.
- **Adaptability:** In our fast-paced world, your ability to adjust to new situations or changes without much stress is a valuable skill.
- **Curiosity:** Your desire to ask questions and learn new things is a driver of innovation and continuous improvement.

- **Networking:** Some individuals are naturally good at connecting with others, but they may not see the value in it. Building and maintaining a network is crucial for career development and personal growth.
- **Patience:** The ability to remain calm and patient, especially in difficult situations, is often underestimated.
- **Storytelling:** The gift of telling engaging stories and communicating ideas effectively is important in terms of persuasion and building relationships.
- **Detail Orientation**: Paying attention to details can seem tedious, but it is crucial in ensuring quality, accuracy, and avoiding mistakes, especially in fields like project management, research, and design.

These skills might seem ordinary, but they are foundations for your success in various aspects of life and work. Recognizing and valuing them can lead to more opportunities.

Here's another way to build your list of superpowers: **what do people ask you to do?** When do people ask you for help? When do others ask you to join in? And what are they asking you for? This is important because that means the people around you think you're good at that thing that they're asking you to do! Take that compliment, accept it, embrace it, and look for more.

And there is much more. Such as **whatever you are recognized for**. If you've earned certifications and awards, if you have some sort of documentation that says you are capable of doing something, you're qualified to do something, add that to your list of superpowers. Include things that maybe you don't love to do, but you are good at them anyway. They're part of your job description. They're things you can accomplish and have accomplished, with success.

What I'm really trying to say is: make this a nice long list of your strengths. Don't be shy right now. Like basketball legend, the greatest of all time, Michael Jordan said, it's not bragging if you can do it.

Here are some examples of strengths from recent participants in my You Own Your Origin Story workshop. These are listed in alphabetical order. You can do it that way or just as they pop into your head or divide by category. The important thing is, can you put your version of these things on YOUR list too?

- Able to make complicated issues more simple
- Adaptability
- Brain is filled with sports trivia
- Continuous Learning
- Collaboration
- Creative
- Digital Fluency
- Embracing Innovation and Change
- Embracing Non-Traditional Learning
- Empathetic
- Entrepreneurial Spirit
- Environmentally and Socially Consciousness
- Financial Awareness
- Global Mindset
- Good at crossword puzzles
- Good listener
- Good public speaker
- Good writer
- Love brainstorming
- Purpose-Driven
- Resilience
- Seeks and supports Inclusivity and Diversity

- Self-Sufficiency
- Strategic thinker
- Tech-Savvy
- Work-Life Balance Focus
- Wry sense of humor

Can you create your own list of 15 or 20 superpowers? Feel free to pick some from the above list if these powers apply to you too. Just write down all you can… then add one more… and one more after that. Once you do, save that file, that piece of paper, or on your phone, keep it with you so you can add to that list as things occur to you. Because what we're trying to do is build this list of things you are good at, things you like to do, the things people ask you to do. These are your strengths. Your superpowers.

Found Flaws

Even Superman has to deal with Kryptonite. We all have our superpowers and we all have flaws and weaknesses we have to overcome. Now it's time to stare our flaws right in the face. It's time to take on our weaknesses. I understand your hesitancy. I'm asking you to do some hard work. To be vulnerable. To trust me and your future mentors. To grow, we have to accept and understand our own weaknesses.

What are your weaknesses? This question might be difficult to answer. After all, who likes to admit their shortcomings? Or it might be too easy to answer if you are self-deprecating or otherwise not so good at promoting your strengths. Another thing is for sure, you should expect to get a question like this in a job interview. "What do you consider to be your greatest weaknesses?" Let's own this. And don't be afraid to grow. We all have areas of our lives, professional and personal, that could use at least some development, some improvement. Let's find our flaws and grow from them.

Weaknesses can come from a number of different areas. You might start by thinking back to your Superpower Portfolio we just created. What did you think about but leave off the list? Here's a way of organizing these thoughts.

- What fits the description of activities you don't like to do?
- Are there activities or tasks you don't feel any positive emotions for? No joy, no excitement, no passion, no anticipation?
- What are activities that drain you of your energy or lead you just to procrastinate?
- What kind of work do you do, but it drags on and it takes longer than it should or longer than it seems to take other people?
- What work does your boss or client or other stakeholder ask you to do that makes you feel uncomfortable?
- And what kind of work simply do other people just do better than you do?

You know, it's all right not to be able to do everything. It doesn't make you weak, and it doesn't make you an imposter. Let's work on this list, even if it stings a little. I think what you'll see is that these weaknesses fall into different categories, and that's where this activity can be really helpful.

One category of weaknesses includes **things you should work on**, and it would be good for you to improve on these things and turn flaws in this category into a new set of superpowers.

This might include items that, even if you don't like them, **you can't get out of doing** it, at least not yet. So you've got to improve, perhaps with practice with better tools with better instruction.

Another group includes activities you can do, but **you need help**... you're better as a partner, a collaborator, a team member, instead of doing the work yourself.

And then, there will be some activities you don't want to do, don't have to do, and you should find somebody who can do them better. Or **just drop them**, if you can. There might be some work that simply kills your spirit, and you have just got to get out of it, or else it's gonna make your heart hurt or your brain throb.

And remember, all the people around you have weaknesses too, and THEIR list may very well include things that are among your strengths. These are great building blocks for collaborations and building partnerships and relationships. In my own work, I find I'm pretty good at generating ideas and good at writing but my work partners are often better at things like statistics and analysis. Does that mean I'm a failure or an imposter? No way. It means I can focus on what I'm good at and find people who are good at the things I'm not.

Just like you created your Superpower Portfolio, now it's time to organize your found flaws into these categories.

- Areas to improve (because you can't get out of doing them)
- Areas to collaborate (because you need help to make them work)
- Areas to shove aside (because you are able to just drop them)

This will leave you with a list of your weaknesses, and also a little self-analysis of why you perceive them to be that way. Even more importantly, knowing where you need improvement prepares you for your next steps: what are you going to do next? What can you offload? What can you work on and improve upon? And what activities do you simply have to accept as something you're not great at... but maybe you'll discover how you can get better.

Points of Parity, Points of Distinction

This will be one of our most important lessons, and I know this from experience and the comments of my students and clients. This section will go a great distance in showing you what you have to offer. There are actually twin concepts at work here. One is called points of parity, and another is called points of distinction.

Parity means things are equal. And what that basically means is that we look at your list of superpowers, and we put it in the context of those around you. I'll give you an example from a client I worked with, an executive coach. I asked him what his strengths were, and his first reply was, "I'm trustworthy." Trustworthy. That is an important strength, of course. We would hope any coach, teacher, mentor, is trustworthy, trusted by their clients, students, and protégés. The thing is, aren't ALL coaches trustworthy, or at least perceived to be that way? It's necessary, it's important, but it's not distinct. It doesn't separate you from others. It's a point of parity, which means it makes you basically equal. It's a minimum requirement.

Let's consider your points of parity by looking at your Superpower Portfolio. Do a quick analysis of each strength you've listed. While these may be strengths, ask yourself if others around you are also good at them. If so, mark them with a p for parity. Don't delete or erase them—just make the note.

Chapter 3: You Own Your Origin Story

In fact, if you left something off your list because you thought, "everyone is good at this," add it back! We want a complete inventory of your superpowers. You wouldn't have your job or career path if you weren't at least somewhat good at these attributes. They're still strengths, but they are your points of parity.

Now go through your list and mark these items with a p. If you find you're putting that mark next to everything, you might be underselling yourself. Give yourself a little more credit!

On the other hand, let us now look at your points of distinction, also called points of differentiation. While you have points of parity and those are among your strengths, your points of distinction are your real superpowers. We're still looking at your strengths inventory. And I hope you've actually continued to add to that list, as you've discovered more things you're good at, that you love to do, that people ask you to do.

Here's a way to tell the difference between points of parity and points of distinction: In my workplace, my faculty hold PhDs, just like me. While having a doctorate is a significant achievement, in this setting, it's simply the norm—a point of parity. We've all worked hard for our degrees, and it's the price of entry for our jobs as professors. However, what sets me apart is being one of the few marketing professors at my school. This distinction becomes even more pronounced when I'm with clients or in community settings where few others have a PhD. Even among other professors, I'm the marketing expert. On the other hand, among other real-world marketing experts, I might not even know as much as they do. In this case, though, my advanced degree becomes a point of distinction again.

Now we're looking at points of distinction on your list. What's special about you? What might help you stand out from the crowd? What can you mark with a big bold D? Like in my example, it might vary depending on the situation. So focus on the different groups you tend to be with, to work with. And we throw aside that humility we had last time. Look at your list of strengths… and keep adding to it.

Let's pick a few examples. You might include among your strengths qualities like fluency in more than one language. Being fluent in Spanish or Polish or Mandarin might not be so special at family gatherings, but in the workplace it might be quite an important distinction. Mark it with a D. How about knowledge of a coding language? Graphic design skills. Negotiation skills. Public speaking skills. Certifications in a particular area. Which of these things are you especially good at? You might not be the best in the whole world at some of the items on your list of strengths, but you are still better than many of the people around you. These are things people ask you to do, because you're better at it than they are. Your talent is there, and it should be recognized. What do you especially love to do? What especially gets your passion going? These are all possible points of distinction. So if last time you used a p to indicate your points of parity, now let's use a big, capital D to show you are pretty outstanding at your points of distinction.

Your Superpowers in Different Scenarios

There are various contexts in which tapping into your superpowers, your personal and professional strengths can give you the strength to succeed. I've listed different kinds of situations you might find yourself in, each one requiring different qualities or a combination of strengths that align with the demands of the moment. Here's how you might use your superpowers in different contexts:

When you are climbing up the walls

I'm not just talking about Spider-man again. This context refers to those moments when frustration, stress, or impatience sets in. You may feel stuck, overwhelmed, or restless. Here, your superpower might be your self-awareness, emotional regulation, or creative problem-solving. It's about recognizing when you're at your limits and finding ways to channel that energy productively, either by taking a break, shifting your perspective, or seeking support from others.

When you want to be strong

Strength, in this context, is about resilience and steadiness in the face of challenges. When situations get tough due to personal hardships, workplace stress, or high-stakes decision-making, your superpower is your emotional intelligence, patience, or determination. It's the ability to hold your ground, remain calm under pressure, and push through adversity with grace.

When you need to be on point

This is about precision, accuracy, and focus. Whether it's in negotiations, delivering a pitch, or problem-solving, being "on point" requires sharp attention to detail and clarity of thought. Your superpowers might include your analytical skills, critical thinking, or an ability to quickly assess a situation and respond appropriately. Here, you're not just hitting the mark, you're nailing it with confidence and competence.

When you want to stretch yourself

Stretching yourself means stepping out of your comfort zone and embracing growth opportunities in your safe zone. This might occur when taking on a new role, learning a new skill, or tackling an unfamiliar challenge. Your superpower could be adaptability, curiosity, or a growth mindset — the willingness to push beyond what's easy and evolve through the discomfort. This is where you grow the most and expand your boundaries.

When you want to be the expert

Being an expert means stepping into a role where your knowledge and skills shine. It could be in a client meeting, a conference, or leading a specialized project. Your superpower might be deep subject matter expertise, problem-solving abilities, or a strong sense of self-confidence. In this context, it's about owning your expertise, knowing your value, and being the go-to person others rely on. You might be surprised how many times you have a level of knowledge or experience on a subject that truly makes you the expert.

When you want to make things happen

When it's time to drive results, your superpowers might be your ability to execute, your problem-solving skills, or your resourcefulness. This is about taking action, whether you're managing a project, resolving an issue, or meeting a tight deadline. It's the moment where your ability to stay focused, organized, and efficient takes center stage. You're the person who ensures things get done and done well.

When you want to be electric

This is when you need to bring energy, enthusiasm, and charisma into a room. Whether it's during a presentation, a meeting, or a networking event, being "electric" means captivating your audience, engaging people, and driving the conversation forward. Your superpower in this context might be your ability to communicate clearly, connect with others emotionally, or inspire people with your vision. It's about creating momentum and leaving a lasting impression.

When you want to be the leader

Leadership requires vision, empathy, and decisiveness. Whether you're leading a team, mentoring someone, or managing a project, your superpower in this space could be your ability to motivate others, communicate a clear vision, or create a positive and productive environment. A leader doesn't just guide. A leader inspires action, builds trust, and empowers others to succeed.

When you want to be a mentor or a mentee

Mentoring is about sharing wisdom, offering guidance, and supporting someone else's growth, while being a mentee requires openness to learning and vulnerability. As a mentor, your superpowers might be empathy, listening, and the ability to provide valuable insights. As a mentee, your strengths could include curiosity, humility, and a willingness to absorb new knowledge. Both roles require trust and a commitment to the growth process.

Each of these contexts as well as the other ones you are facing, or will eventually, call on different facets of your Superpower Portfolio, and understanding when and how to use your strengths can make you more effective, adaptable, and successful.

The Origin Story You Own (Your Elevated Elevator Pitch)

One point of this chapter and the entire concept of You Own Your Origin story is to show you that your strengths are real, your flaws can be overcome, and you are more than just a bystander: you are on a Hero's Journey toward control over your career. An important next step is your ability to articulate what you have discovered about yourself and share your story with others, including employers and mentors.

A good elevator pitch is a well-known and powerful way to convey who you are, what you do, and why it matters. Personal pitches serve to clarify your unique story and build confidence. By distilling your key strengths and experiences into your pitch, you affirm your value, helping to overcome imposter syndrome. An effective pitch also opens doors for networking and mentorship by making it easier for others to see how they can support or collaborate with you. It demonstrates self-awareness and helps you connect with new opportunities, giving you the well-deserved confidence to take control of your career and relationships.

So here's the next step. Write your origin story. We'll take this in two parts. Part 1, just have fun and continue your (super)Hero's Journey. Write out your origin story in just a paragraph or two. Here's an example from a recent YOYOS workshop participant:

"Armed with a head full of organic chemistry equations, Lee embarked on a great journey to the tropical land of Singapore to conquer the world of medicine. But after being bitten by a radioactive confidence cockroach, Lee realized it was not the best place to be. Running with almost superhuman speed from the overwhelming AFEL monster (Asian Familial Expectation Leviathan, Lee's arch-nemesis), Lee used the skills of humor, discipline, and intelligence (along with Clark Kent-level charm) to crisscross the world, fighting the dark powers of unrealistic expectations and perfectionism. What is next for our hero? Only time (and the completion of an MBA) will tell... but earning the title of "Nurse" has a nice ring to it."

As fun and thrilling as Lee's story is, I do have to admit that in a more professional setting, like a job interview or networking event, this fantastic tale might catch your conversation partner off guard. Yet, it might have been this whimsical approach that helps you to accept your experiences, recognize your validation, and yes, help you own your origin story! Plus, it's not hard to translate your origin story into something more professional. In a meeting, when asked for a self-description, Lee might say:

"My journey began with a deep dive into organic chemistry and a goal to study medicine in Singapore. However, after reassessing this path, I realized it wasn't the right fit for me. Drawing on humor, discipline, and intelligence, I have navigated through global experiences and overcome the pressures of high expectations and perfectionism. Now, as I work toward completing my MBA, I am focused on my next challenge: becoming a registered nurse and continuing to make a meaningful impact in healthcare."

How could Lee do this? How can you do this? It might be simple enough for you to step back, change from superhero mode back into your civilian identity, and translate your story. If you prefer, you can also use an AI platform like Gemini or ChatGPT, with a prompt like: "Can you convert this superhero origin story into something I might share at a job interview or elevator pitch?" As always, when you are using AI, be sure to read through the output to make sure you are comfortable with what the computer created. After all, it's YOU having these interactions, not a computer.

For another perspective, here's my origin story:

"Possessing only an MBA and lacking work experience, DAVE ARON wandered desperately through jobs in retail and online shopping mall management. Facing an existential career crisis, Dave sought wisdom from the mystical marketing magi, gaining the power of… a PhD.! Thus empowered, he transformed from a marketing practitioner to a marketing professor, teaching classes, mentoring students, and serving clients as Doctor Dave!"

This can be translated into:

"After earning my MBA, I explored various roles in retail and online shopping mall management but found myself searching for deeper meaning and a more impactful career. This led me to pursue a PhD in marketing, transforming my career trajectory from practitioner to professor. Today, I not only teach and mentor students but also work with clients, applying my practical experience and academic expertise to help solve real-world marketing challenges. My journey has been about continuously evolving and finding new ways to add value through education and strategic thinking."

You own your origin story. Now write it and share it.

The Foundation for What Comes Next

Your origin story is crucial because it reflects the real-world challenges you've overcome, showcasing the resilience and perseverance that shaped who you are today. It explains and validates your journey, providing context for where you are now and the person you've become. By reflecting on your path, you see how your success and growth are not just deserved but earned. Owning your story also brings clarity, helping you recognize how far you've come. Each step has played a role in building your strengths and identity. It's not simply about reaching a destination but appreciating the growth and learning along the way. Your origin story also serves as a personal guide for navigating future challenges. The obstacles you've faced weren't just barriers; they were critical in developing your resilience. Armed with this understanding, you can approach new challenges with confidence, knowing you have the strength to overcome whatever comes next.

Your journey has given you a clearer sense of purpose, values, and goals, along with a sense of gratitude and responsibility to the important people who supported you along the way, including mentors, friends, and family. Their influence has shaped your success. Acknowledging this creates a powerful sense of accountability. By sharing your experiences, you can guide others on similar paths, paying forward the support you received and fostering growth and community. Your origin story is a testament to your achievements, proving you've earned your place through hard work and personal growth. Embracing your origin story empowers you to take full ownership of your strengths and capabilities. By recognizing your unique skills and qualities, you can confidently shape your future, knowing you have control over your narrative. Your origin story is more than a reflection of the past; it's a tool for driving your future impact.

Chapter 4: Can I Grow or Do I Go?

You've been reading my origin story in some great detail, and I hope at this point you have at least thought about your own origin story too, and how you deserve the good things that have happened to you so far in your career. If you're still reading this I imagine you have more questions about your career and mentorship, and you are looking for more answers. So far I've written about many of the bumps I experienced during what the calendar might call the first half of my career to date (roughly 20 years... a long time!), but I've shared relatively little about the second half, the one I'm currently experiencing, or about how (comparatively) smoothly this second half has gone (roughly the past 20 years... also a long time!). In between the first 20 and the last 20 was one crucial, career-transforming year and I'll talk about that soon. Symmetry!

Before we get there, I want to look at what we've covered so far and what we are about to talk about next. You've seen how difficult the workplace can be. Now don't get me wrong, I know I'm not working in a mine or in a factory. I'm not a gear-cutter by trade. I don't work in a food processing plant. I'm not working in a boiler room, literally or even figuratively, with me shoveling coal or depending on the next sale to make sure I can feed my family this week. But a lot of what I faced during that first half of my career really does apply to many different kinds of careers:

Challenges at Work:

- **I faced high pressure and unrealistic expectations:** My colleagues set tight objectives and deadlines that were both unrealistic (Mandy) and unexpected (Chet), leading to stress and feelings of inadequacy.

- **I was in an unsupportive work environment:** Some colleagues and their relationships made it difficult to challenge decisions (Mandy and Ronnie); some leadership simply made it impossible to do my job (Whit and Pablo, Whit and Lena) or even understand what was expected of me (Whit and TechFirm). This hindered my progress and job satisfaction.

Lack of Control:

- **Career Uncertainty:** Feeling lost and unsure of my career path, I struggled to find direction and advancement opportunities (TechFirm). This caused a sense of aimlessness and dissatisfaction.

- **Personal Struggles and Career Transition:** The challenging transition from a previous job (Eastland) to the next (TechFirm), with my hoped-for mentor getting fired (Jim) so soon after I started, kept me off balance for a long time. Then, at that same job, I was asked to make up fake data to impress a client as part of a research project, which drove me to my career change, from corporate to academia. Throughout these years, I felt unsettled and out of control.

Desire for Growth:

Need for Career Development and Mentorship: While I recognized the importance of control, I did not have the background or wisdom to seek help, formal or otherwise, in order to gain direction for my professional growth. This absence of a mentor to provide guidance during my challenging time made it hard to navigate difficulties, and hard for me to make informed decisions.

And that more or less summarizes the first 20 years of my career.

With this in mind, the purpose of this chapter is to offer you a definition of mentoring. You have come this far, so that seems like the least I can do. We'll define the term and I'll illustrate the meaning of mentoring by sharing some examples, some good ones and some not-so-good scenarios of where I encountered opportunities to be mentored. Note that I wrote "opportunities." That does not mean I took advantage of them.

What is Mentoring

Mentoring is a supportive relationship in which a more experienced individual, the mentor, guides and fosters the professional and personal development of a less experienced individual, the mentee or protégé. This is what we might call the "classic view" of mentoring as defined by Kathy Kram (1985). The classic view puts the emphasis on the transfer of skills, knowledge, and support, political, social, and psychological. In this sense, mentors act as advisors to younger, less experienced others, offering career guidance and helping mentees and protégés navigate the challenges in front of them.

This seems like a good time to address the labels "mentee" and "protégé." These terms are similar in meaning and are often used interchangeably, even by me. The word mentee is more general and apparent: someone who is mentored. The word protégé suggests a deeper relationship, almost like an apprentice. Both terms are appropriate for describing someone receiving mentorship, but "protégé" suggests a more intense and committed relationship. If you can understand my using one term when I should maybe use the other, I will extend the same courtesy to you. By the end of this book I promise we will be speaking the same language!

Mentoring thrives on several key elements. The first of these core aspects of mentoring involves a knowledge transfer, where the mentor shares their expertise and experience to guide the mentee's growth. This is complemented by a supportive relationship built on mutually-held trust and encouragement. Together, the mentor and mentee work toward the mentee's goals, ensuring a meaningful path forward. While mentoring structures can be formal or informal, the most rewarding relationships are those that prove mutually beneficial, with both parties gaining valuable insights and connections. Yet mentoring might be seen as a one-way street, with brilliant wisdom and knowledge flowing from the mentor, generally older and more experienced, to the young and novice mentee. We can call this a top-down approach.

Well times sure have changed, I say as I wait for my daughter to show me how to fix my frozen smartphone. Enlightened and modern folks like us know mentoring goes both ways now, what you might call a reciprocal learning experience. Both mentor and mentee benefit from the exchange of ideas, perspectives, and experiences. It's not necessarily that the student has become the teacher, but it's more like I know a lot of things from my 30 plus years of experience and you know a lot of other things from being a digital native who can seemingly send a text message without actually touching any of the letters on your phone. And any (old) person who doesn't appreciate what others have to offer is really missing out.

There is a term for the relationship in which the younger person is a mentor to an older mentee. It's called reverse mentoring and that term is wrong. It's ageist. It's still mentoring in every sense of the word. If you have more experience than I do in, say, recording and editing a podcast and you generously come to my assistance by sharing your wisdom with me, you are the mentor. We'll talk a lot more about this later, as we discuss managing your mentoring relationship. In the meantime, since so many other people use the term "reverse mentoring," you can use it too. But I still think the word "reverse" is not needed.

Back to top-down mentoring. There are also two broad kinds of models of the traditional approach to mentoring. One is formal mentoring. Here, I am describing a structured approach to mentoring in which an organization provides a mentor to a younger or new employee. Or, instead of pairing one mentor to one mentee, the company might assign more than one mentor to the employee, or even have a group of mentors from the employee to choose from.

First Day/Worst Day

This brings us back to my first day at Chicagoland. One announcement, of course, was that they were moving the goalposts, by making the emphasis of my job research more than teaching. As a tenure-track faculty member, we basically have three overarching responsibilities: teaching, research, and service. It's hard to quantify the exact percentages of each for a given job. At what we call a "Research 1" school like Michigan, where I got my PhD., my non-scientific guess is something like 20% teaching, 70% research, and 10% service. My more current and still non-scientific guess about where I work now might come close to reversing those numbers, more like 60% teaching, 20% research, and 20% service. At Chicagoland, I thought it would be more like that last set of figures, but they swapped it out on my first day there. And it just felt like it was 100% teaching, 100% research, and service whenever asked.

The second major announcement on my first day was that a new mentoring program was now in place for our department of twenty-some faculty members. Each junior faculty member, (Assistant Professors like me), would be matched to a team of three senior faculty members (Associate or Full Professors, already tenured and therefore older, wiser, and secure in their jobs) to serve as mentors during the pre-tenure stage of their career. That sure sounded like a good idea for a needy youngster like me, except for the fact that when this announcement was made, the senior faculty were not smiling. As I looked around the room, most were looking down. Nonverbal cues! Body language!

My trio of mentors was a supergroup, consisting of three men: one in his sixties, one in his fifties, and one in his forties (by my best estimation at the time, as a naive 34 year old) – Willie, Rodney, and Tracy, respectively. Three tenured marketing professors, each entrusted with guiding me through the terrors and travails of the early years of my career, leading me toward my eventual promotion to tenured professor status. It didn't quite work out for me that way. I'm going to tell you much more about Willie, Rodney, and Tracy later on. For right now, let me summarize my relationships with each in a few words, with more details to follow in a later chapter.

Willie: He sat in a little, windowless, smoke-filled office at the opposite end of the hall. When I started at Chicagoland, Willie was in his early 60s but seemed much older, he seemed to speak only of his impending retirement. He still had not retired by the time I was pushed out. Willie would respond to direct questions but had almost no other presence in my life. He didn't initiate contact or conversations with me. I never knew what to ask him. These are all obstacles to finding and nurturing a productive relationship with a mentor.

Rodney: How could I know so little about a person whose office was two doors away from my own? Rodney seemed to enjoy working with my junior faculty colleagues, at least the ones who would share their data with him and let him be the lead author on their collaborations. I do understand the economics of that kind of transactional approach, but since I didn't have data of interest to him, he had little time or use for me. He was always curt and walked by me whenever our paths crossed.

Tracy: I actually got along well with Tracy and we interacted frequently. However, I was put on alert early on when I heard another senior faculty member refer to him as a "slimy snake-oil salesman" in front of me and another colleague. And this was coming from another professor! Such an unprofessional thing to say. My memories of my conversations with Tracy center around how he would end our conversations by asking "do you know how much I would get paid for this" advice, referring to how he bills his consulting clients. I never did ask. Maybe that was his way of emphasizing just how valuable his wisdom was, but I didn't pick up on that back then.

Let me pause here to accept responsibility. As a matter of fact, as disastrous as this formal mentoring program was for me, EVERY OTHER junior faculty member who started within a year of when I did made it through successfully and earned tenure. Everyone but me! What a perfect, perfectly toxic opportunity for me to blame others or blame the system for what happened. But I blame myself. I accept responsibility. The data is there. But talk about a formula for imposter syndrome! Whatever system

Chicagoland put in place, whether objectively good or bad – it worked. For them. For everyone else. Not for me.

But my goal is to help you and people like us, so I'm not talking about everyone else. I'm talking about me. And I'm talking to you. Any situation that works for everyone else but not for you is very clearly not the right situation for you to be in. Superman would not have been Superman had he stayed on Krypton. He would have just been Kal-El, maybe following in his dad's footsteps and becoming a brilliant scientist. Or maybe he would have chosen a different path, lived his own life, and become an artist. No wait, their planet exploded! So let's get back to the topic at hand. My old workplace did not explode, it's still there, and there was no instance of my father or mentor or anybody else lovingly placing me in a rocket ship to escape. The fact remains, it was not a good fit. I knew this from Day One and I did not leave, I did not seek a better fit, until they told me that I had no other choice but to leave.

A Mentor Appears

Would a different mentor, a better mentoring relationship than what was offered by Willie, Rodney, and Tracy have helped? I worked closely with another senior faculty member named Phil and I'll use this example to describe the benefits of that kind of individual-centered mentoring that offered more to me than the mandated tri-mentoring plan. That formal plan, with my superteam of Willie, Rodney, and Tracy, was what we might call top-down and structured mentoring. My relationship with Phil was so much more robust and beneficial. We can call this top-down, organic mentoring. Not a forced relationship, but one that evolved more naturally.

Chapter 4: Can I Grow or Do I Go?

Let me describe Phil to you through this short, intense example. Phil and I co-taught the undergraduate honors in marketing course. I would present lectures on marketing strategy to our best marketing students, guiding them toward the creation of a marketing plan for a real-life client. Phil was a believer in the case method and if you've never heard of Professor Kingsfield from the 1973 film The Paper Chase, please take a moment to look up a video clip from the movie. Professor Kingsfield. You'll find it.

Phil was very much like the character portrayed by Oscar-winning actor John Houseman. He was absolutely feared by his students until after they graduated. Phil was the professor who would lock the doors the moment class started. If you were late, you would miss class that day. Phil would, on more than one occasion that I saw, make students cry as he (fairly) criticized their presentation. However, once the tormented youngsters stepped out of our classroom and into the real world, their opinion of Phil and his Kingsfieldian approach (I'll wait if you haven't looked him up yet) changed 180 degrees. Now, dealing with colleagues, clients, and bosses, and the demands of being a grown-up, the alumni appreciated all Phil had put them through. His lessons were painful but valid and necessary. Phil provided them. He was fine with that.

For this particular semester, our classroom client was a local charity that gathered and distributed school supplies for underprivileged children in the Chicago Public School system. The organization was the Walter and Connie Payton Foundation. If you are from Chicago or follow the professional National Football League, you know of the legendary Sweetness, Walter Payton. Payton's stature as among the best ever to play is so enduring, and his legacy of philanthropy and community service so beloved, that the annual Walter Payton

David Aron

NFL Man of the Year Award is given by the NFL in recognition of a player's commitment to philanthropy and community impact. Payton had died just a year or so earlier. While his widow, Connie, also was prominently featured in the name of the charity, most people could not identify her even if they saw her. Of course Walter was a different story. In Chicago and around the country, he was revered like few other celebrities before or since. We were so fortunate Connie agreed to work with us, representing an exciting opportunity for our undergrads to learn, to experience so many different areas of non-profit marketing with such a recognizable name.

To be clear, Walter Payton had not been a business professional, and Connie was not either. Like so many famous people, they dedicated their name and the power behind it to a worthwhile cause. So when Connie came to visit our classroom, she lit up the room with her charisma and her passion but was certainly not about to impress anybody with her business acumen. That's okay. That's what her foundation was there for, and, I hoped, the members of our class. The backstory of how such a prominent name was even in our classroom to begin with is a lesson all by itself, and we will come back to that when we discuss comfort zones.

Connie came to our campus in Chicago to meet our students and talk about her organization. She did not bring spreadsheets, tables, or business terminology, she brought excitement and words of hope for the children whose lives she improved. Connie brought love. According to their mission, the foundation was dedicated to "helping abused, neglected, and underprivileged children in the State of Illinois. We strive to help boost these children's self-esteem and give them a reason to believe that tomorrow can be different.... That tomorrow can be better!"

Chapter 4: Can I Grow or Do I Go?

The students connected with her genuine affection and dedication to her cause, and she left the room to a standing ovation, not the typical polite applause that generally concludes a client visit. This was especially satisfying to me and promised a unique educational experience for our students. But later that afternoon I heard "What is THIS?" shouted from our office mailroom. That was Phil, who walked into my office seconds later. "Did you get one of these?" he shouted.

"I haven't checked my mail since lunch…"

"Read this." Phil demanded, still at a shouting volume, as he handed me the letter. "What do you think?"

I read the professionally-worded letter from one of our students about our client. The student was unhappy about this project. This woman was not a professional, not a business person, the student wrote, and it was unclear how much the class could learn from somebody who was merely a figurehead, the wife of the original figurehead, and didn't know anything about the world of business in general, let alone the basic functioning of her organization.

"What do you think, Dave?" Phil asked as I scanned the bottom of the letter.

"No signature. Seems kind of gutless."

"Unprofessional." Phil concurred. Or, more accurately, corrected me.

By this point, our little conference had drawn the attention of colleagues around us. Phil took the letter back and started showing it around to the three faculty members who had joined us in my office. "Do you recognize this handwriting?"

"Now we're starring in a detective show," I quipped. "We could narrow it down to about 24 people." That was the size of our class.

So what was the problem? Neither Phil nor I had any issue with a student not appreciating, understanding, or even liking the client based on our first meeting. It happens all the time, as recently as this past semester in my current job. Let's face it, some students want to work with Procter & Gamble for their class projects, others want to work with the gray-haired but still ultra-hip solopreneur opening an independent bookstore down the street. And there are plenty of options in between. Most students will remain open-minded about their impending learning experience. But apparently, not all.

Phil continued. "Here's the difference. If we demand a confession, it becomes us against them, right? That would make for a long semester together. And if we just make an announcement to the whole class, it's too easy to ignore, especially if 'someone else' did it."

Demand a confession? Wow, Phil was tougher than me. I never even would have thought of that.

"So what do we do?" I asked those gathered in my office, all with about the same limited amount of experience as I had. Clearly, another kind of class was now in session.

Phil noted that the student wrote in the letter "several of us feel the same way." "That part may or may not be true," Phil observed. "Personally, if it were 'several' of them, I'm even more disappointed none of them had the courage to put all their names on this letter. But I've seen enough cases where it was just one person hiding behind some made-up friends."

Chapter 4: Can I Grow or Do I Go?

"Okay," I replied, "What do we do about this unhappy camper?"

Phil placed the letter on my desk right in front of me. "I'll be in my office. Let me know when you have some ideas."

With that, Phil left, as did my three fellow junior colleagues. Thanks for all the help guys.

But Phil... Phil understood the situation. At his age (twenty years older than me), with his experience (lots, compared to my almost none), he'd seen a lot of classroom conflicts. And on the surface he and I, as co-instructors of this class, were in the same boat. But in the bigger picture, we absolutely were not in the same boat. Phil was a senior faculty member, tenured, fairly invulnerable to the politics of the department or institution, respected by his peers and past students, and not concerned about what our current students wrote about him on their course evaluations. He could wait until the youngsters went out into the real world for the plaudits and appreciation.

I was pretty much the opposite of all of those things. Now in only my second semester, I was under all-consuming pressure to finish my dissertation or, conceivably, I would lose my job. I left Michigan with "ABD" status. That means "all but dissertation," with only the successful completion of my written dissertation (never guaranteed) standing between me and my PhD. But, as I was frequently reminded by my chair Chet and others of all shapes, sizes, and professional standing in our department, I was expected to complete my life's work (at least, up until that particular point in my life) within the next several weeks. So I was not bulletproof like Phil but rather felt like I was wearing a big heavy target instead. Forget about respect from peers or students: I was still recovering from some less-than-stellar course evaluations from last semester, my first at this job. Why is Phil making me do this? I should be working on my research instead!

Here's why: Phil was a good mentor. Phil gave me guidance. He helped me set up guardrails. He explained the consequences of making poor choices and with that, left the task of making the right choice up to me. He knew the pressure I was under and also let me know I couldn't ignore this other vital element of my work - teaching - and I couldn't ignore the students who depended on me.

I stared at the letter. The kid's just frustrated, I thought. He's young, he doesn't know how to ask for help, but that's all he really needs. Someone to listen. He wants to be heard. Yeah, I was thinking about myself too. You figured that one out too, I'm sure. I didn't know what to do, and I didn't want Phil to have to solve this problem for me.

I had an idea. I grabbed the letter and ran to Phil's office. But, first a stop at the copying machine, located right next to the mailboxes where Phil discovered the letter a few minutes earlier. I made 24 copies of the student's letter.

Phil was sitting at his desk, reading the *Wall Street Journal. How does he have the time?* "Phil, I've got it."

Without looking up from his paper, he replied "Got what?"

I put the letters on his desk in front of him. "A little handout for our next class meeting."

He looked up over his glasses. "Go on…"

"Let's start class by reviewing the client's visit. Let's spend half an hour with an open floor discussion of what the students understand about the project and our expectations.

Chapter 4: Can I Grow or Do I Go?

Phil put the paper down, a small grin starting across his face.

"Maybe our letter writer will speak up if we give this opportunity. I think that's all he or she really wanted, to be heard."

"And if he or she doesn't?"

"Then we pass out these copies of the letter. Not to embarrass anyone, but to turn it into a lesson about professional communications. And to see who else feels the same. I don't think they know what a great opportunity this project is for them to use their marketing skills..."

Phil finished my sentence, as he often did. "... for a good cause." Phil looked at me. "Sounds like a plan." He went back to reading his paper.

And that's what we did. Most of the students were thrilled about the project and the opportunity to become teachers, marketing mentors, to our client. Many had questions and concerns about our big-hearted but inexperienced partner. We debated different approaches to this project, which was what the course was all about. Some students used the open forum to express their uncertainty about the project. In terms of content and scope, our letter writer likely found that the "several of us" who felt the same way were not nearly as vocal about their concerns, if those classmates even existed at all.

After some discussion, I passed out the copies of the letter. Phil and I watched for the students' reactions. We noticed as several turned their eyes toward one student, Anthony, who had been among the few expressing negative thoughts during our recon session. Maybe he tried to recruit others to his letter-writing campaign. Perhaps other students felt that same level of insecurity that might lead one to submit a letter like this anonymously (especially given Phil's strong and harsh reputation and my utter lack of one). The conversation turned toward our offerings of reassurance and the need to sign the letter, the importance of seeking a voice and standing behind your beliefs. We earned that teachable moment I had hoped for. I still use this post-meeting reconnaissance approach in my classes today.

After class, Anthony walked up to Phil and me. He had learned a lesson that day. He apologized for writing the letter. Phil looked at Anthony. "Do you believe what you wrote?" Anthony paused. "I believed it then. I'm still a little unsure, I guess."

"Then don't apologize for the letter. Don't apologize for speaking up. Just be more professional next time. Stand behind your words," Phil said.

"And," I added, "give us time. This is a great opportunity. We'll take care of you."

The Halftime Show

While we're talking about football… we have arrived at halftime. Not of the book, there's much more in store for you in this and the following chapters. This is the start of what I call the halftime segment of my career. More on that in just a moment.

My relationship with Phil started when I found myself co-teaching this course with him, and then it evolved and deepened during my years at Chicagoland and even beyond. I certainly learned a lot from Phil but not even he could save me. He made me a better teacher but he couldn't help me with my research. This illustrates a point I will make in greater depth later on, the need for more than one mentor to address the many needs for guidance we all have. I am still amazed at how many people I talk to think all you need is one mentor. Of course, there is no need for monogamy in mentoring, whether you are the mentor or the protégé. Actually, more people seem to think you don't need a mentor at all. If you are in either of these categories, I'm glad you're reading this book. And if you know someone else who thinks they don't need or can't find a mentor, please share this with them when you're done.

As I mentioned above, it is around this point, a few years after that classroom incident, that what I've been calling the first half of my career comes to an end. I was called into Susan's office. She was now the Chair of the marketing faculty, having replaced Chet a couple of years earlier. Sue and I got along well, much better than Chet and I ever did. Was she a mentor to me? Let's call this another missed opportunity. A big miss. Sue was well-established in her career and was familiar with the kind of research I was interested in. She knew personally many of the researchers I admired. Let's all shake our heads together in disbelief for another possible mentor in my universe, one I never reached out to for the kind of help I needed. The point here is this was just another relationship, one of many relationships at Chicagoland, I simply did not take advantage of.

Sue called me into her office to tell me she just received a report from Willie, Rodney, and Tracy. Their consensus opinion was that with only one published article, I should not even bother going through the tenure approval process. This process was an arduous one, involving creating portfolios for all members of the university and departmental appointment committees to evaluate. The feeling was they already knew there was no way within a year's time I would be any more qualified to earn tenure than I was at that moment. It was left to Sue the Department Chair to break the bad news to me. I think I took it like a champ.

I was not surprised. A lot of times you might hear stories of people feeling a sense of relief upon being fired. I think I felt some relief or at least some closure but my big concern was this: I had moved my family 300 miles from Michigan, where my wife had a good job, to Chicago. My wife still had a different good job and my kids were in school but now I was a year away from being unemployed. That's how the system works: they give you a year to finish your work, to get your act together, and find another job.

While I'm in this reflective mood, let me make another observation. As I write this, I've gone back to look up some of the people I've been mentioning, just to see where they are now, how their careers have moved along since our last contact. A few of them have passed away in the 20 years since what I've declared the midpoint of my career, the transition from Chicagoland to Dominican by way of Northern Illinois University. Willie, the first of the triple-mentor program I was part of at Chicagoland, passed away a few years ago. Here is how one of my former colleagues described him: "Willie was the 'grandfather' of our department. He was a mentor that cannot be replaced. He worked with numerous faculty members on research projects, and helped junior and senior faculty succeed throughout the tenure and promotion process."

Does that sound exactly like what I needed or what I saw for myself in Willie? What did I miss? Where was Grandpa Willie when I was struggling with my research? He was right there, in his smoke-filled shoebox of an office. He was helping my young colleagues but not me. I am guilty of judging a book by its cracked and timeworn cover. And I was not ready or able to do the work required to build that relationship. You have mentors in your universe, right now. You don't have to be told, but you might have to tell them. You might have to do what I did not do

Chapter 4: Can I Grow or Do I Go?

– go into their office, or send an email, and start the conversation. And they might not all be willing to work with you at this particular time, and they might not all be able to help you. Mentoring relationships are not guaranteed to work; I've got a whole chapter on this coming up. But if you have to go through a smoke-filled room to find Willie, or if you have to go through a Willie, a Rodney, and a Tracy in order to get your Phil, then it's up to you to get started on that path. And don't forget about Sue. And Willie. He apparently DID have a lot to offer, if only I had known to ask or known how to ask.

So that was it for Chicagoland. The afternoon I met with Sue was the start of the transition point between the first half of my career and the second half. Here's one other thing I didn't do during my years at Chicagoland in addition to not taking advantage of the many mentors that might have been available to me: I hadn't built much of a network. There are a lot of universities and colleges in the Chicago area and I knew almost nobody. I used to blame the fact that I lived 35 miles away from campus for my lack of connections but that's just an excuse, and not even a good excuse. I could have built a network closer to the suburb I lived in as well as building one in Chicago but I did neither.

When I got home that night after talking to Sue, I met my wife in our kitchen to tell her the news. My wife is in a different profession all together but she has a few diplomas in that home office of ours too. I knew she could relate. In the years since we returned to the Chicago area, her employer had been purchased by another company, which was in turn swallowed up by an even larger company. So she understood stress at the workplace. But neither of us had ever been fired like that before.

Denied Man Walking

What can I do now? Find another job, of course. But I felt like a dead man walking. I couldn't even imagine going into the office on Monday, let alone asking anybody for help. Let me pause here for another aside to tell you just how wrong that attitude was. Look, I was not caught embezzling. I had actually been asked to do worse things at TechFirm. That's right, I'll talk more about this in chapter 5. For now, just let your imagination run wild about all the ways professors could lose their job. I didn't do any of those things. I did not get into a fistfight with the department chair, neither Chet nor Sue. I didn't call any of my colleagues a "slimy snake-oil salesman." I had become a good teacher (thank you Phil) but not a good-enough researcher. And it would be a safe guess to say that nationwide, roughly a third of junior faculty members are denied tenure. Just a guess.

There are some schools where tenure is incredibly elusive, and others where earning tenure is almost a given. Plus, let me add: I was not denied tenure. Thank you, Sue. But that "six years and out" on my resume was going to be awfully revealing to those in the business, those I would hope would hire me. And I just didn't feel comfortable asking anybody else for help. I was too embarrassed. Not Rick, I must be the first of his students ever to not get tenure (I'm pretty sure that's not true but I have no proof). And not Phil. I didn't even want to know what he would think of me. I was just a guy who only published one paper when he should have published… I don't even know… more?

There are always possible drawbacks to any interpersonal relationships, including those related to mentoring. One of my biggest mistakes was not fully entering these relationships, even when they were imposed upon me from above like with Willie, Rodney, and Tracy. Phil and I had a wonderful relationship, even after I left Chicagoland University, all the way until his passing. I was drawn into that relationship, by the proximity created by our team-teaching experience. My lessons from Phil illustrate the importance of mentorship that goes beyond the formal, assigned kind. That kind of thing didn't work for me. But Phil's guidance and support not only improved my teaching skills but also equipped me to handle a challenging classroom situation. It showed me the value of open communication, constructive criticism, and fostering a safe space for students to voice their concerns.

In the bigger picture, there were so many opportunities for mentoring relationships beyond Phil but I was too wrapped up in my own situation to take advantage of what was right in front of me. I didn't realize how much help I needed until it was too late and I was shown the door. These lessons, along with the many others I learned during this pivotal time in my career, would pave the way for the transformative "halftime" period I'm about to discuss. Now it's time to delve deeper into the concept of mentorship, explore different mentoring styles, and see how finding the right mentors can make all the difference in your professional journey, as it did in mine. I'll address this by looking at a fork in the road... the very forks in the road that I experienced at Eastland and again, just a few years later, at TechFirm. No silverware for me at Chicagoland U., but still some lessons to share. Should you stay or should you go? And while this decision is yours to make, we will explore the role of mentoring relationships in this decision.

Chapter 5: Growing or Going I: The Fork in the Road

My years at Chicagoland saw me desperately in need of help, of mentoring. I received some guidance from Phil, which was a top-down approach and grew organically. Even though Phil passed away a few years ago, his wisdom still serves me well to this day. My lack of successful experiences with Willie, Rodney, and Tracy, as well as several others from that era of my career, are little more than footnotes now. Still, they illustrate how a structured mentoring program means very little if the participants - mentor and mentee - are not willing to invest their talents and abilities in the creation of a meaningful relationship. Sure I blame them, but more than that, I recognize I did not do all I could to build these relationships and so I share some of the blame.

At Chicagoland, I was never in a position to make the career decision of whether I should stay or I should go. At Eastland Mall I did have that choice, and also could have decided to stay at TechFirm. Eastland Mall was one of many shopping centers managed throughout the United States by developers Jacobs, Visconsi, and Jacobs (JVJ). There was a fairly defined mall management career path laid out by JVJ. A young assistant mall manager like me would start at one particular mall, which for me was Eastland. Under the tutelage of the mall manager, the assistant would focus their attention on either the marketing or on the operations side of running the mall, while still participating in all aspects of mall management. The marketing or operations assignment was generally a function of the employees' strengths.

My experience fit this template: Whit's strength was in operations management, so my marketing background provided a healthy complement. The best managers were adept at both, thanks to their years of experience in running the property and dealing with their tenant store managers. The assistant manager would typically stay a year or so at the first mall, learning and supplementing their knowledge through their experiences and through working with their manager. After that year, the assistant would be transferred to a second JVJ mall, somewhere else in the United States, depending on need and on the role that was to be emphasized. For me, after my first year focusing on marketing, my second stop would likely have been at another mall, taking greater responsibility for managing the operations of the mall, and possibly working under a more marketing-savvy manager. That might have been nice. We never got that far.

As we moved through the summer of my year at Eastland, the issue of my career path and next move became increasingly relevant. To the credit of Whit and Pablo, they knew that since I had a wife and small child, I wanted to stay as close to Columbus as possible. See, I DO have something nice to say about them! Remember Bob and Carrie, my fellow assistant managers in Pablo's region? Bob was in his second stint as assistant manager and so, according to the template, his next stop would be to run his own mall. At the time, that sounded like such an attractive path, such a strong proposition to me. But Bob couldn't leave until a mall manager position became available for him, and turnover was much less frequent at that level. Carrie, on the other hand, was in her first year like I was, and had a marketing background like I did, and couldn't stand her manager either. Could she and I switch malls? From what Carrie would tell me about her boss, I much preferred to stay with the devil I knew than the devil I didn't.

Since moving was not an option, part of me tried convincing myself I could handle Whit for another year. And that I could handle Pablo for another year. But handle Whit and Pablo together? So toxic. But that status quo seemed bearable and I did enjoy my work with our mall tenants. And speaking of toxic, I had become used to not getting any support from Lena and I really didn't know any other sort of relationship could exist. So Whit and Pablo decided I could stay at Eastland for my second year as assistant manager. That was nice and they did not have to do that.

What a lovely story! That was all true, but only the outside. On the inside, coming to work every day was miserable. I was miserable. My only solace came from talking to the store managers and employees, most of whom hated their jobs too. My soul and my ego both still hurt from Whit's rejection of the Hoops for the Hungry event that Carrie and I had developed a few months earlier, shut down along with just about every other idea I had. And Pablo, therefore, didn't see much of my creative side. He decided that I was as boring as Whit. Early that summer I had started to actively seek another job, without any success.

Weigh Your Options

The decision to stay or leave your job can be motivated by all kinds of different reasons. It might be motivated by lack of joy, recognition, or potential for growth like my situation at Eastland. Sometimes you or your family relocates. That's what happened to my wife, as she left a perfectly suitable job in Michigan to come with me to Chicago. Sometimes, like my subsequent experience with Chicagoland, the decision isn't yours at all. Conversely, a suitor might offer you an opportunity you can't refuse, and you accept a lateral move or even a promotion with another organization. And sometimes you just have no choice but to leave. Here, I don't mean no choice like Chicagoland pushing me out the door, but a more dramatic event that happened to me and hastened my exit from TechFirm. I had no choice but to leave.

My career at TechFirm probably could have lasted for years and years. I did my job, supporting our sales reps, staying out of Mandy's way, fulfilling her promises to clients when I could, and cleaning up her messes when I had to. While the rest of the mall team (sales reps, account support specialists, and database editors/coders) were a fairly stable unit, I was still bouncing from manager to manager while serving the mall group (matrix management: I am not a fan) until finally Arnold took over our Electronic Shopper. Arnold was a skilled and successful sales manager, coming from another department within the company to finally provide the kind of leadership we had been missing since Jim, the guy who hired me, had been fired three months after I started.

A fellow Ohio State grad (him, a bachelor's degree, me, my MBA), Arnold was just a year older than me but with several years of valuable experience under his belt. He and I got along well from the start, and our relationship grew to the point he would invite me to join him for lunch with his other friends from around the company. If we look at our relationship in terms of mentoring, Arnold was sharing his resources, his social and political capital, with me. He was inviting me to industry conferences, along with him and our sales reps. My role at these events was still that of support, of coming up with creative ideas on the fly to help my teammates close their deals. He was stepping into the role that had been missing from my career. Arnold was a leader and a mentor to me. And I was an idiot.

I guess the best analogy I can come up with is that I had a new toolkit and I didn't know how it worked. I became impatient. A few months into Arnold's term as our manager and a couple of years into what was my second job, I was seeing some friends from grad school and some coworkers at TechFirm get promoted. "Why not me," I wondered. When I brought up the topic with Arnold, his response was that he was still figuring things out and there was no place to promote me to in our Mall environment. This news was offered to me in the same spirit as our friendship but I took it all wrong. After all, my position, which was now finally taking form, was created by Jim. Why can't we create a new position for me to rise up to? My interpretation of Arnold's reply was that I should seek my promotion through another department within the company, much as the path that had led Arnold to our Mall group. No, that's not what he said, but that's what I heard.

TechFirm was more than just The Electronic Shopper. In these early days of a very limited Internet (the word was capitalized back then), TechFirm was one of the very first ways for a computer user to access the web. Very few businesses even had websites, if you can believe that. A great amount of TechFirm's revenue came from some key sources besides the rent paid by Mall stores. This included serving as a contractor for H & R Block's instant tax refunds (in fact, they ended up purchasing TechFirm), along with the company's subscriber base. To attract subscribers, TechFirm paid fees to partners and content providers like AP (Associated Press), UPI (United Press International), Reuters, Microsoft, IBM, Borland, and 3Com Corporation.

These relationships were managed by my colleagues with offices that had walls that actually reached all the way up to the ceiling. I started to quietly schedule meetings with managers from other groups within TechFirm, informational interviews to learn more about what was going on outside of my silo. I left little doubt there was an intentionality to these conversations, that I was on the prowl and looking for a greater opportunity. Let me take a moment to offer you a little mentoring, which may very well be applied to your decision to stay or go. Consider strategy and tactics. These two terms are often used interchangeably but unlike me, say, switching between "mentee" and "protégé," which are quite similar if not identical, "strategy" and "tactics" are very different.

Strategy refers to big-picture planning, long-term goals, and a desired direction you want to take your career or your company. Career wise, I had little mentoring up to this point, and there's no substitute for having a mentor or two or three or more that can offer you that kind of big-picture perspective young careerists simply don't have. Tactics are more action-oriented, specific steps taken to execute a strategy. "Rise to the level of Electronic Shopper Manager" would have been a career strategy, and the tactics are steps I might have taken to make myself ready to be, and deserving of being, promoted to Mall Manager. These tactical steps might have included traveling more frequently on sales calls with Tom and our other reps. Perhaps I could even spend a year as a sales trainee. I certainly would have had to learn how to work better with Mandy and Ronnie. I would have had to find a way to show I was capable of making decisions and taking actions that improved TechFirm's bottom line. There was a long list of tactics I could have pursued if I wanted to serve the strategy of gaining more responsibility at TechFirm. I just shared an example of a good strategy (become a manager) and strong tactics (gain skills, build relationships). On the other hand, I lived out an example of a weak strategy (look aimlessly, desperately for a different job) and poor tactics (random interviews with supervisors I barely knew), and, crucially, not including my would-be mentor Arnold in the conversation. That is a recipe for failure.

Here's something else to know about just about any workplace: secrets don't remain secret for very long. And something else: it is unprofessional to poach talent from another supervisor or department. That doesn't mean a promotion cannot cross departmental lines... in fact, that's how many opportunities are found. But I was offering myself up to anyone who seemed the least bit interested and now it just seemed pathetic. And moreover, I was putting these other managers in that position of poaching an employee (me) from one of their peers (Arnold). It did not take long before one of the managers I met with told Arnold about what I was doing behind his back.

Like I said, I was an idiot. Poor strategy, poor tactics. And Arnold's feelings were hurt. My activities placed a chill on our relationship. Life went on but so much of the color was gone from my daily work. Mandy seemed more and more insufferable. And then, as my situation seemed to be at its lowest and most hopeless point, Ronnie called me into her office. Arnold, who reported to Ronnie, was in there with her. This is a scary picture. The only thing scarier would have been if someone from Human Resources had been in there with them. With an empty box. Or with a security guard. As I walked toward Ronnie's office, I could only think of one outcome to my impending visit with her and Arnold: I'm being fired for my betrayal. I might as well grab a box and clear out my cubicle and get ready to leave. I didn't think I deserved it, but I knew I did something wrong and the way things had been going lately, maybe this was inevitable.

Surprise!

I was not fired that day. I was not fired at all. Instead, with Ronnie listening in, Arnold told me Tom was close to bringing in a huge client for the Mall and they needed me on a special project. To offer you some context, the clients, our virtual tenants, in our Electronic Shopper paid to be included in our shopping offering. The more web pages they required, or the more complicated their offering in terms of the creation and maintenance of their digital space, the more "rent" they paid. Tom, they told me, was on the verge of bringing in an American automaker as a client. At that time, that meant one of the three Michigan-based, global automakers: Ford, Chrysler, or General Motors. Whichever company it was, they wouldn't sell their cars directly, but would instead use the Mall space as a showroom while selling swag like shirts, gloves and key rings and scheduling test drives. Sure, now you can buy a car on your phone but believe me, at that time, this was pretty cutting edge stuff. Ronnie joined in to tell me she had hired an independent automotive marketing research consultant out of Michigan and I would be his right-hand man, helping him understand how the Mall works and, crucially, helping him design and execute a survey to measure just how excited our hundreds of thousands of subscribers would be to visit the automaker's store in our Electronic Shopper.

Are you kidding me? A key project? Build a new skill set? Represent the Mall with a consultant and a major client? Execute a plan to increase the bottom line? THAT, my friends, is at least a couple of steps toward getting a promotion. Now, as you read this, I wonder if Arnold had something to do with this opportunity. Did he arrange this? Did he put in a good word for me with Ronnie? Was I the very first person he thought of when Tom shared this exciting news? Okay, pump the brakes,

Chapter 5: Growing or Going I: The Fork in the Road

Dave. But still, this goes beyond being a mentor to what you might call an advocate or a sponsor, someone (Arnold) who takes a role in finding opportunities for a mentee (me) they would not be able to find by themselves. At that time, however, I never thought about any of that at all. Still worried about keeping my job, I said yes without even considering how this new responsibility would affect the other aspects of my work.

So add this to your list of mentoring tips... you are keeping a list, right? When you are asked to take more responsibility, go in with that "Say yes" mentality, as you must in order to grow. However, make sure you aren't biting off more than you can successfully chew. And if you are concerned you might be overextending yourself, work with your boss to set priorities. Fortunately, Ronnie and Arnold made it clear this was going to be my top priority (in addition to, you know, everything else I was already doing to support our clients) and they set up a meeting with me and Sandeep, our one-man marketing research consultancy. The impact of this assignment on my career cannot be overstated. This was going to be huge. And it was huger than huge. Just not in the way I expected.

Sandeep was just a few years older than me and was working as a freelance marketing research consultant out of Michigan. He was good at marketing research, and was at that time on hiatus as a doctoral student at the University of Michigan. Remember that place? I mentioned it one or two times earlier. At that time, though, I actually knew very little about U of M, other than they were the intensely hated rivals of Ohio State, where I had earned my MBA. It would not be wise to wear your maize and blue in Buckeye Country. Sandeep was the researcher, and really did the work in developing a survey to be sent around to a group of TechFirm subscribers. I learned at his side, honored to be his student and occasionally be asked for my opinion on different questions and versions of the survey as we built it. Even as I continued my other work in supporting the sales reps and the mall, this was my needed diversion. I threw myself into this project. The color was back in my life! Before long, as Tom continued to nurture his automaker relationship, our survey was ready to be emailed to several thousand of our subscribers.

Our subscribers were pioneers at the dawn of the Internet. In the early, early days of the world wide web, the process of using the internet was quite a bit more complicated than it is now. When I was a TechFirm, access to our Electronic Shopper, as well as the company's other products and the internet itself, involved purchasing software, from a store, in the form of floppy disks (and later, CD-ROMs), then installing them on your computer (not your phone), then hooking up a modem to attach your computer to the outside world (no Wi-Fi) through your phone (a landline), hoping nobody else was using the phone at the same time, and finally, slowly, loudly, connecting to what few offerings existed online. At TechFirm, we charged about 20 bucks for our Starter Kit software, and we charged users for subscribing to our service. These subscribers were, in general, Uber-nerds. Proto-nerds, the first, earliest form of nerds of the computer era. Our subscribers liked computers. They liked the hardware and the software. They liked books, especially books about computers. And, interestingly, they liked ordering shoes.

And the Survey Says...

Sandeep and I pored over the results of our survey. And the survey showed that TechFirm members were just not that interested in learning more about our prospective client's cars. We brought our results to Ronnie and Arnold. Ronnie was not pleased. "Guys," she began, "Tom's doing everything he can to win a huge account for us. Please do this again. I want new data in a week."

In the world of academic research, the data is precious and methodology is important. Research papers are published (well, not by me while I was at Chicagoland, but in general) with the intention that another researcher can use that particular study as a springboard for a new project, continually advancing the scope of understanding about that particular field of knowledge. We stand on the shoulders of giants, in terms of mentors and in terms of research, too. Sandeep shared this wisdom with me as we began tinkering in the commercial (not academic) world of research by modifying the questions and gathering thousands of email addresses for a new set of respondents within our subscriber base. Ronnie did not give us a lot of time to collect and analyze new data but Sandeep wasn't worried. He knew he built a strong study. We sent it out, and in almost no time, the new results started pouring in.

Sandeep and I analyzed these new answers from new people, and ended up with very similar results to what we had seen a week earlier. This new subset of respondents showed once again our subscribers were just not that interested in cars on TechFirm. Now, with the right amount of creativity and work from our Mall team, we might have been able to turn this automaker, and any client for that matter, into a success story. I can't even imagine what Mandy would have promised the automaker I would do for them. But like I mentioned, we sold a lot of men's shoes in our Mall. However, this prospective client didn't want to spend hundreds of thousands of (early 1990s) dollars on something so new, so uncertain, like ecommerce.

We brought the news to Ronnie. She was upset. "Gentlemen, I'd like you to run this survey one more time. Come back in a week. And this time, please do not waste the client's time or waste my time." Sandeep and I thanked her and left her office. I wasn't quite sure what she meant, but Sandeep knew. He knew exactly what she meant. Sandeep walked me back to my cubicle and we sat down. "Dave, my friend, that's it."

"'That's it'"? Like "Eureka! I've discovered gold!"? No, not at all. Sandeep didn't say "that's it" with enthusiasm, like he just discovered the solution to all of our problems. This was a tired, sad "that's it."

"What do you mean?" I asked.

"I can't work for her," he replied. Now you know I've had my struggles with Ronnie and especially with her bestie Mandy, but it was never enough to make me leave. Actually, maybe it should have been enough to make me leave. And I had half-heartedly tried to find another department to call home. But I was still there. I still didn't understand why Sandeep was so blue. "Dave... don't you get it? She wants us to make up data." No, I certainly did not get it, not at that time. I just looked at him in disbelief. "Don't be naive, Dave. She wants this client so bad she wants us to make up data and present it to them like it's real. She wants us to make it look like the subscribers want to see them in your Mall."

This just did not compute, no pun intended. Maybe a little bit intended. "Can't she get in trouble for that?" I asked.

"No," Sandeep replied. "She'd pin it on us. If anyone even found out, which I doubt," he continued. "So I'm done. I can't be part of this. It would ruin my career. I'll see if she's still in her office."

I looked at Sandeep as he stood up and I bowed my head. "Dumb question, Sandeep: What should I do?"

"Quit. Just quit like me."

He said it so matter-of-factly. "No, I can't just quit like that. Come on, I've got a wife, we've got a kid and another is on the way. And I don't want to lie. I don't want any part of this either. I guess I'm just screwed."

"You could go to grad school."

"I've got an MBA that's not doing me any good right now."

Sandeep paused. "No, you could do this. Marketing research. You'd be good at this."

Welcome to the crucial cubicle conversation that changed my entire career.

Crucial Cubicle Conversation

Sandeep continued, giving me the big-picture perspective of pursuing a marketing PhD in the early 1990s. Tuition would almost certainly be covered by my work as a research assistant. I would spend a few years learning a whole lot about very little, as the saying goes. There are a few schools within a reasonable drive from Columbus (including Ohio State) if I could not move my family. Sandeep said I should start looking at academic marketing research journals to see what interests me as a long-term project (that became the dissertation I mentioned earlier) that would serve as the basis of my career. Maybe if the timing is right we would be fellow students, together at Michigan, if I could get in and if I wanted to go there. Wouldn't that be fun?

My head was spinning. My dream project had turned into a nightmare and then into this…whatever this was. Sandeep went from my cubicle to Ronnie's office and quit the project. He left the building. And I spent the rest of the afternoon beginning the process of exploring just what the heck Sandeep was talking about. The more I looked, the more I liked. Sandeep could tell that just because I was good at helping him with our research project, maybe this was the right move for me.

My wonderful wife and growing family supported this idea (and supported me throughout this search and throughout my program). So now, once again, it was time to quit my job. This kind of bouncing around from job to job (or in my case, career to career) was not as prevalent back then as it is now, and this move I was executing was not as simple as just going from Eastland to TechFirm. Back at that time, the only reference point I had for a career change was going from high school to college, and that was one anticipated for years.

Moving away from the mall was great for me, but starting at TechFirm, as you saw, was not easy. And up until the day Sandeep left, I thought I was finally starting to figure out how to grow into a job, how to create an identity. A personal brand. I was going to be the guy who helped Tom bring a Big Three major American automaker to The Electronic Shopper. The more I explored the possibility of pursuing a PhD, the more excited I became. I loved marketing, I loved advertising, I loved these types of elements of my work. It was all the other stuff, the fights over scarce and artificially scarce resources, I could not figure out. Surely that's not what life would be like as an academic (spoiler alert: it is very much what life is like as an academic... but I still like it better than my old life).

There is a bit of an epilogue to this automotive motivation for my career change. There was some immediate fallout from Sandeep's decision to leave. First, Ronnie was a little mad at me but very, very mad at Sandeep as he walked out the door.

Chapter 5: Growing or Going I: The Fork in the Road

Ronnie then told Arnold to let our Detroit prospect know that we needed one more week to evaluate our results and we all looked forward to sharing some exciting news with them. But no: they got tired of waiting for us and backed away from the deal. So now Tom is mad, Ronnie is mad, Arnold is mad, Sandeep is gone, and I just wanted to learn more about going back to grad school. The remaining months I spent at TechFirm are a blur to me. I kept afloat at work while applying to seven different doctoral programs including, of course, the University of Michigan. As I write this, I'm thinking "isn't this a strange way to wrap up a chapter about staying at your current job." After Eastland and TechFirm, I sure don't seem like an expert at staying and growing, but I have learned a few things over the past few years, both in general and about staying at my current job.

First, a few reflections about my time at TechFirm. I really owe Arnold a debt of gratitude. The more I think about our relationship, the more I can see he was truly trying to help me build a career at the company and at The Electronic Shopper. I may never know for sure if the entire marketing research with Sandeep project was from his recommendation, or if Ronnie just didn't think I had enough to do with my time, but it was clearly a life-changing opportunity. Note too that the project absolutely did not turn out as anybody had originally hoped or expected. The idea was to win a huge new account and the outcome was that we didn't win the account, the consultant stormed out of the building, and I was gone soon afterward to become a doctoral student.

Another note about Arnold's benevolence and my ignorance is that at one point during my last months at TechFirm, he introduced me to a new Mall colleague named Prue. I still remember once that Arnold told me that lack of personnel would never stop us, and if we needed someone he would find someone. That's so, so different from what we deal with today, where everybody seems to be doing the work of two people or more. So I didn't even ask directly, but the next thing I know, Prue was brought in, he told me, to help me in whatever I needed. So, basically my assistant, even if she didn't report to me and even if Arnold didn't tell me this directly. And Prue was great.

Another mentoring issue, though: I had not supervised anybody since my senior year in college (please don't include Lena here) and that was more along the lines of telling people where to hang up flyers in the student union. So I could have used a little good old-fashioned professional development and training to make that relationship work. And maybe that was part of the problem, part of my problem, that I needed advice to be spelled out to me directly and in large, bold letters before I understood it. That might explain my ignorance until the time when Sandeep directly told me what he thought I should do. That's another couple of lessons for mentors and for mentees. Mentors: don't assume your protégé understands what you're telling them. Have a sense of that person's level of development. And mentees, here's your lesson: if you're not sure… ASK!

And another thing: I continued my unfortunate habit of acting like I wasn't allowed to contact people once they left my workplace. I simply did not stay in contact with people whom I no longer saw in my day-to-day life, like Jim and Sandeep and my Ohio State business professors, and my friends from the Eastland Mall stores. Keep those connections alive, my friend. I had Sandeep's TechFirm email address, but he might have deleted it the second he got home. No surprise, really, he did not leave the organization on the best of terms. But that's just an excuse. I never reached out. Sandeep lifted me out of the hole that my early career had become. He would not be the last person to provide me with a mentoring intervention.

Chapter 6: Growing or Going II: Tools for the Mentor and the Mentee

The decision to stay at your current job or leave that job for a different one is not an easy one. At Eastland, even though I enjoyed collaborating with Carrie from across town, I could not stand the people I was working most closely with. Yet I really enjoyed the work and there was a clear, well-trod, and defined career path that might have led me to a better situation at another shopping center. Those were valid reasons to stay, not to mention the uncertainty that is always involved in taking a new position. I chose to leave, and when I told Whit, his first response was "Was it something I did?" Oh, Whit. Whit, Whit, Whit. It was mostly what you didn't do. You didn't believe in me or in my ideas, You didn't mentor me at all, and you certainly did not support me or give me any guidance in my situation with Lena. From Eastland, I moved to TechFirm, thinking I was going to connect with Jim, an inspiring boss I saw as the mentor with whom I could work and learn, only to have him disappear three months later.

In this chapter, I am going to share a number of tools you should have in mind as you build your career, whether you choose to stay and grow, or you choose (or are forced) to go. I'll list them here, and then illustrate them throughout this chapter... and beyond.

- Self-Advocacy
- Strategic Thinking
- Partnerships
- Networking
- Self-Reflection
- Examining Your Comfort Zone
- Seeking and Taking Advantage of Opportunities.

For example, my move away from Eastland was an example of self-advocacy. Self-advocacy means ensuring your career progresses forward, that your work and contributions are recognized, and that opportunities for growth are not missed. Self-advocacy is crucial to staying in control of your career, rather than passively receiving what others offer you... or throw at you. My years at TechFirm were a different flavor of disappointment and somehow the lessons I learned about self-advocacy at Eastland disappeared. I stayed at TechFirm, wandering aimlessly for a few years, and there too, a better situation might also have been on the horizon if my research project with Sandeep had turned out better. This was another case where self-advocacy meant leaving a bad situation to find one better aligned with my goals. So I left TechFirm and made the huge pivot from corporate to academia. Once again, I chose to go. And I went, moving from Ohio to Michigan with the support of my family but, professionally speaking, on my own.

This was me trying to take charge of my career. Having a mentor would have made a huge difference. Mentors offer valuable career advice, help shape your goals, and boost your job satisfaction and skills. They can use their insights and experience to help you overcome challenges, build confidence, and achieve success in your field. At Eastland I found no such support, and at TechFirm I didn't see mentors were right in front of me. However, as I demonstrated, finding and maintaining a good mentor relationship can be difficult. It takes effort, support, and sometimes a bit of luck to find the right match. And then even once you've connected, keeping the relationship strong requires ongoing commitment from both sides. Busy lives, shifting priorities, and personality clashes can all make it hard to keep in touch and manage a relationship effectively.

As I wrote above, there were certainly opportunities and reasons to stay at both my Eastland and TechFirm jobs. There are ways to make your decision to stay work out well for you. For example, at Eastland, I could have grit my teeth and dealt with Whit and Pablo and Lena for one more year or so, hoping to get promoted to another mall. The result of that plan might have involved a very long commute or moving to another city in order to stay with the company. At TechFirm, the path was not so clear. Remember those informational/job-seeking interviews I conducted behind Arnold's back? Learning more about your workplace is always a good idea. Building relationships outside of your own department is also smart. And there's nothing wrong at all with seeking to rise within your company, even if the path is more jagged than straight. See? A plausible idea handled poorly by my sneaking around and not working with my boss as an ally. And now, looking back, I think I really had little choice but to leave TechFirm. Even though the project with Sandeep shriveled away almost as soon as he left, perhaps I impressed Arnold enough to get another high profile project. On the other hand, my relationship with Ronnie, always quite tense (for me, anyway) thanks to her close relationship with Mandy, was further tarnished now but for all the right ethical reasons. I failed her loyalty test and I didn't know if she would trust me to do her bidding in the future. The right way to grow in your job is with your boss as a partner in the process. A good leader, a good mentor, wants you to grow to the point where you get promoted and become a leader in another role.

If you've been keeping track, you see I accumulated quite a few poor mentoring and leadership experiences during the first half of my career, running from Eastland to TechFirm to Chicagoland. There have also been a couple of strong, positive relationships that demonstrated examples of mentoring in action, but do you know that old saying "when the student is ready, the teacher will come?" In those cases, particularly with Phil at Chicagoland and Arnold at TechFirm, I simply was not ready to receive the wisdom shared with me. This student was just not ready. So at this point, let us examine some of the real benefits of having a mentor, the things I missed by not recognizing the opportunities in front of me. We can also look at some of the things I might have done differently, or that my bosses might have done differently, to create stronger mentoring relationships and opportunities for growth.

What Are the Benefits of Having a Mentor?

We've already seen numerous instances during the first half of my career where I longed for a mentor. Someone to show me what I didn't know or to warn me about the mistakes I was about to make. A future version of me, or at least some aspect of me. Relationships with one or more mentors offer benefits that can lead to professional and personal growth. One such benefit is simply the growth in your skills and competencies as mentors share their knowledge and expertise with you. This can lead to an increase in your self-efficacy, or the confidence and self-assurance that come from guidance and encouragement from experienced mentors. That would then bring about opportunities for career advancement, where your mentors and advocates provide insights to help you navigate your career path, make strategic decisions, and maximize opportunities for professional development. Additionally, creating a network inside and beyond your workplace will expand your connections within your industry. This would provide for you diverse perspectives, advice, and support crucial for your growth and long-term success.

Improved Skills and Competencies

This learning is part of a dynamic process where you, as the mentee, will acquire and refine essential abilities under the mentor's guidance. A strong mentor will provide personalized direction that accelerates your professional growth. This might include technical skills, leadership development, or specialized industry knowledge. As you saw through my experience with Phil at Chicagoland, collaborative projects and ongoing feedback will help you gain practical experience and the proficiency necessary to excel in your current role and prepare for future career opportunities.

Increased Self-Efficacy

Mentoring plays a pivotal role in boosting your self-efficacy, that is, your confidence and self-assurance. I can tell you first hand that people early in their careers or at a transition point may start with uncertainties or self-doubt. Through the support and guidance of a mentor or mentors, you gain a clearer understanding of your superpowers: your strengths and how to leverage them effectively. Mentors provide you with encouragement, constructive feedback, and opportunities to apply your newfound skills, gradually building your confidence in handling challenges and achieving goals. This increased self-efficacy extends beyond immediate tasks to overall career aspirations, empowering you to take on new responsibilities and pursue ambitious objectives with greater assurance.

Career Advancement

The increased skills and increased confidence that emerge from your work with a mentor serve as a catalyst for career advancement. You will gain strategic guidance and insights into navigating your career paths, whether that path is linear or completely the opposite. Mentors also offer insights beyond your headlights, with perspectives on industry trends, organizational dynamics, and potential career trajectories. Crucially, as Arnold might have done for me, mentors also advocate for their mentees within their professional networks, recommend them for new roles or projects, and provide introductions to influential contacts. This not only accelerates your career progression but also equips you with the knowledge and skills to adapt to changing professional landscapes and achieve long-term success.

Network of Mentors

With these benefits in mind, let's take a look at some of the ways you and your mentors can help you prepare for, arrive at, and maximize your success from your decision to grow into your current job or go on toward your next one. From one crucial turning point in my career to the next, my experience with mentors had evolved from none at Eastland, to missed opportunities with Arnold but a crucial conversation with Sandeep at TechFirm, to more missed opportunities at Michigan, to lots of bad mentoring experiences but one good mentor in Phil from my years at Chicagoland. But I was done at Chicagoland. I had a year to continue working there while I searched for my next job, which was standard operating procedure for people like me seeking tenure but not earning it.

What Are the Risks of Not Having a Mentor?

The reason I was asked to leave Chicagoland was for not creating, let alone publishing, enough academic marketing research. That's on me. This is despite getting my PhD at one of the finest research institutions in the world, and working closely with one of the most honored marketing research scientists in the world. Believe me, it hurts just typing those words, even after I've experienced many successful years and career moves since then. But it's important to recognize this kind of self-reflection, this self-examination, can yield a big payoff. It can also reveal other thoughts and other realizations that did not occur as they were happening. While I have been focusing on my own inability to see past my headlights and take advantage of the opportunities in front of (or alongside) me, I have to admit I was at a bit of a disadvantage at Chicagoland. I had a family. On the day I started at my new job in Chicago, I had a wife who also worked and we shared three beautiful children, at that time aged nine, six, and three. The older two were in school and an after-school care program, and the youngest in daycare.

Those of you reading this who have kids in daycare, or were kids in daycare, know where I'm going with this. Every day, there is a limited window of time to drop the kids off and pick them up at the end of the day. My wife and I developed a nice planning model. Every semester, I would know which days I had to be on campus, 35 miles from home in Chicago, and at what times. With this in mind, she would then let her administrators know so they could plan her monthly work schedule, working in various locations several days a week, generally 12 hour shifts that almost always lasted longer. With THAT in mind, we would know who had the responsibility for dropping off and picking up the kids on a given day. It was not easy, but we made that system work. And we were fortunate that whenever one of the kids had to stay home, one of us was able to be with them. I appreciate the space to work from home that came with my teaching schedule, and my amazing wife's flexibility and ability to find colleagues to work her shift when necessary.

There were times my department chair Chet (the one before Sue) decided department or committee meetings had to be held with little advance notice. This would make the system my wife and I were living under shudder. On one such occasion, in the middle of the afternoon, Chet told a group of us on a marketing department committee that we needed to meet the next morning at 8 am. This was well before digital meeting platforms like Zoom or Microsoft Teams or Google Meet existed. There was Skype and WebEx, but we didn't have access to those options. And I felt like I was in no position to decline this sudden invitation. But that next day was a day my wife worked and I was planning on staying at home, with dropping off and picking up responsibilities. So I confided in Lori, Chet's assistant, that I would not be able to make it to the 8:00 meeting. Did she think that would be okay with Chet? She told me she didn't know. I was going to have to figure something out and fast. If my wife couldn't find a substitute… I guess I could call in sick?

Lori did not keep my message a secret for very long. As I checked my email one last time before heading home, Lori poked her head into my office and told me Chet wanted me to stop by his office before I left to catch the train. The train that would allow me to get home in time to get the kids. Chet knew I had talked to Lori about missing the meeting. He then questioned my dedication to my job. My dedication to my profession. He questioned my ability to succeed at Chicagoland. He seemed to be taking my parental responsibilities as a personal attack. I felt sick… but not the "call in sick" kind of sick. More like the "crawl inside a hole and die" kind of sick. Like watching our family system as it started to groan and buckle under pressure. I explained my situation and Chet angrily invited me to skip the meeting, warning me not to let this happen again.

Now you might be thinking Chet is one insensitive guy and I agree. He was to me, anyway. You might also be wondering if Chet had any kids of his own and the answer is yes. Two adult children with his first wife, and a younger child with his then-current, stay-at-home wife. Okay, how about the other twenty or so people in the department? That's a lot of people. Didn't any of them have young kids that they needed to watch? Here, the answer is no. No member of the marketing faculty at this time, young or old, had such parental responsibilities. To a person, every other member of this group either had no children, had adult children, had an au pair, or had a stay-at-home partner. The concept of having to go home or stay home to attend to your kids was truly extraordinary and otherwise unrepresented in my department.

A couple of years later, when Sue told me not to even apply for tenure, it was a decision six years in the making. It was not just my dispute with Chet. Phil couldn't help me. Willie, Rodney, and Tracy wouldn't or couldn't help me. Phil was not surprised to hear the news. He either suspected it was coming or, as a senior faculty member who worked closely with me, might have been privy to the information. His advice on what to do next was sparse. He had been at Chicagoland U. for decades. I don't know if that had anything to do with it, his wishing me well but offering little guidance for whatever was coming next for me. Maybe the whole situation made him uncomfortable, considering how closely we had worked together in the classroom. Maybe this was his Professor Kingsfield personality rising up to put a wall between us, instinctively expecting me to figure things out for myself as he did in the earlier situation with Anthony. I know I didn't really know what questions to ask. I already knew how to read the help wanted ads (paper and digital) and go to conferences. That's how you find a job, right? Well, of course it helps but definitely is not everything. And I had not established much of a network to lean on either.

Opportunity Knocks

Moving toward the end of my one-year exit ramp from Chicagoland, Larry, one of my already-tenured young colleagues in the marketing department there, had some interesting news. He told me he had a professor friend who had just left her job at one school to take a job at another. This was weeks after that year's jobs conference had come and gone, and Northern Illinois University's marketing department had a sudden, unexpected need for a consumer behavior instructor. Larry said I should look into this. NIU is about 70 miles away from the big city, a rural state school compared to the downtown Chicago location of Chicagoland. And I lived almost exactly halfway in between the two of them. Incidentally, the job Larry's friend accepted was at a university very close to my house, another school I had applied to. So I guess I could cross that one off my list, yet another job that apparently I was not going to get. But that's how it goes, and as one job offer closes, it looks like another one opens up. I had an opportunity now and I had to take advantage of it. On Larry's recommendation, I reached out to Denise, the chair of the marketing faculty at Northern. She invited me over for an interview.

From NIU's point of view, there was not enough time to put together a full-scale search for this woman's replacement. They needed to quickly find somebody that could teach her classes in the coming year, and during that year they would embark on a search for a full-time, tenure-track replacement. "Lines" for a full-time, tenure-track faculty member are a scarce resource. I'm not sure if that's how it was at NIU in the mid aughts compared to how it is now at Dominican. At my current school, there are many hurdles to jump over when it comes to hiring faculty. In my department, if a marketing professor left, for any reason, we would have to apply to the University-level higher-ups to replace that person, in competition with all of the other departments throughout the entire university who also had to replace somebody.

I assumed that maybe the folks at NIU must be desperate to hire at this relatively late date, and their desperation, combined with my feelings of loss and hopelessness, did not lead me to feeling confident as I approached this opportunity. But you know what? That simply is NOT the way to approach any situation. Opportunities like this come up all the time in all kinds of different contexts. Would I have felt any differently if I thought instead that NIU was simply expanding their department? That they anticipated more students for the next semester than originally expected and needed more hands on deck and more instructors in the classroom? What difference does it make? Reasons for the decisions we make, that others make, are often so multi-faceted and context-dependent it's impossible to know the whole story, especially from the outside.

You Don't Always Have to Be First

To support my point, here is a short list of people who were not the first choice for their eventual role yet achieved great success. Let's start with examples from the world of business like Steve Jobs returning to lead Apple, and then Tim Cook as his successor. Eric Schmidt at Google. Sheryl Sandberg at Facebook. None of them were first choices for their positions. In entertainment, can you imagine anybody other than Harrison Ford, as Han Solo and as Indiana Jones? He was not the first choice for either role. Could anybody other than Hugh Jackman portray Wolverine? Not the first choice. How about Bryan Cranston as Walter White in Breaking Bad? Not the first choice. And one of my favorite examples, from the world of sports, is my fellow Michigan Wolverine Tom Brady, universally recognized as the greatest and most successful NFL quarterback ever. Brady was the 199th overall pick in his college draft. He was not a heralded overall number one pick. Instead, he was told at least five times by every team in the NFL that they didn't think he could play for them. Don't worry about when you're selected. As long as you're given a chance, you have an opportunity to succeed. And I was getting a chance.

This opportunity at NIU provides an opportunity to talk about stepping outside of your comfort zone. How do you define your comfort zone? You know that phrase, we hear it all the time, usually preceded by "you've got to step out of…". And what does that mean? We'll look at this in greater detail in chapter 10, so for now, think about a circle. That circle is filled with what you do every day. What you're good at. What makes you comfortable. That's your comfort zone. Staying at Eastland, or staying at TechFirm, those might have counted as two kinds of comfort zones. If you stay in your comfort zone, it can become like a merry-go-round. A nice gentle pace, some mind-numbing music, and you may find yourself moving around but not moving forward.

Leaving TechFirm to start grad school in Michigan, that has to count as stepping outside of my comfort zone. How about you? Are you willing to step out of your comfort zone? As I hope you've realized by now, you can still be safe outside of your comfort zone. This may not be the case 100% of the time, but it is true surprisingly often. Think about it. What are some things you have done and achieved that, looking back, you realize maybe you actually did step outside of your comfort zone? And what are some things you have been hesitating to do that, if you think about it, may be pretty safe after all? You've seen other people take chances, high or even medium probability of success-type chances, and you can too.

Chapter 7: Mentoring Intervention

It is because of the mentoring intervention I experienced in 2005 that I am writing this book for you in the first place. I know the word "intervention" is a loaded one, evoking thoughts of timely and possibly traumatic interventions to save people suffering from alcohol and drug addiction. I am not appropriating or changing that meaning or in any way disrespecting or minimizing actions and programs meant to help people in need. I am referring to the very definition of the word intervention as an action meant to interfere with an outcome or course of events, to prevent harm and improve outcomes. The word intervention can also be applied here. Nobody can deny the importance of your career, of my career, and of careers in general. And as 2004 turned into 2005, and my career was at a low point with little hope in sight, I was helpless. I felt powerless. And my career was saved by that very kind of action, an intervention that interfered with the path my career was on. Interfered, in a good way.

To fully appreciate the impact of what I'm about to share with you, the impact of mentorship on my career, I have to tell you about Keith and his role in my professional journey. As I will spell out in more detail in a later chapter, Keith was the founding editor of the journal that published my one paper. When nobody, not even Phil, was able to offer me guidance, I sent an email to Keith and told him about my sad situation at Chicagoland. Within hours, he responded with a three-page response (when printed out). The message was one of reassurance and hope. He told me he was proud of me for taking on the kind of research - consumer grudgeholding - he helped to create but very few others had explored. "That took courage," he wrote. This meant the world to me. With his one email, he offered me a lifeline through my stressful period of being lost in the academic wilderness.

I felt like a failure, leaving TechFirm a dozen years earlier and dragging my family hundreds of miles and then hundreds of miles again only to force them to watch me miss my opportunity. But with his letter, Keith advised me, mentored me, and believed in me. At a time when my trust in those who worked with me was at rock-bottom, I was offered a kind of selflessness and compassion I had never experienced in the workplace. Even with my admittedly missed opportunities with Arnold, Phil, Sue, Willie, and who knows who else, I could not imagine such… caring. If not for that letter, I don't know that any of the events that transpired in this current chapter would have happened. I don't know if I would have trusted anybody… or if I would have believed in myself. And now an opportunity was presenting itself to me in the form of a visiting faculty position at Northern Illinois University, a school many of my friends and relatives had attended decades ago, but one that was a mystery to me. At this point I was desperate enough to explore this new possibility, and with Keith's injection of support, I was confident enough to pursue the opportunity with all my might.

From City Mouse to Country Mouse

My drive to DeKalb for my interview was a culture shock. After several years of living in huge college towns, then moving to one of the largest Chicago suburbs, and then regularly commuting to downtown Chicago with its population of over 2.5

million people, I could scarcely comprehend this town in the middle of the farms and cornfields, a town with less than two percent of Chicago's population. I was in the country now. Lots of rolling acres, lots of livestock, and a big, beautiful, sprawling university campus that dominates the town instead of just climbing up and down one street corner like Chicagoland. Maybe everything is different here. One thing that was not different is that, like a lot of state universities, Northern was primarily a research institution, and if I couldn't handle the research obligation and demands at Chicagoland, there was really no reason to think I could handle it here or anywhere else. But that was a worry for another time. The position I was interviewing for was that of a Visiting Professor. The person hired for this job would be a one-year stop-gap for the marketing department, replacing the woman who left abruptly. A Visiting Professor would focus only on teaching her courses and a few others, with no expectations for conducting research or even serving on committees. This person would be there only to teach. I hoped this person would be me.

To get to NIU, I had to drive five miles north to the Interstate, and then go west onto US Highway 88, past Mooseheart, past Sugar Grove, Kaneville, and Maple Park until I got to DeKalb. If I were going to Chicagoland, I'd go east onto 88 instead of west. So of course I turned to go east. Force of habit. What a way to start the drive. The wrong way. Luckily, not only was I nervous enough to go the wrong way on the highway, I was nervous enough to leave about 30 minutes earlier than I really needed to so I had time to reverse course. I made it to campus in plenty of time, and even though Northern's 800 acre, 64 building campus is much more complex than Chicagoland's 11 story building in Chicago, my years at Ohio State and the University of Michigan (roughly 1,700 acres and 3,000 acres, respectively, if you're keeping track) brought a welcome sense of space and big campus familiarity. The business school and its marketing department are housed in the beautiful Barsema Hall. I felt like I was walking into the future even though I can't really say it was more futuristic or tech-forward than Chicagoland's facilities. Maybe I felt like I was walking into *my* future. I found my way inside and walked through the main plaza to the marketing department office suite. The student worker guided me toward a conference room where, dressed in my suit and tie, I sat down to wait. I wondered who I would speak with. I had studied Northern's large marketing faculty on their website but my mind was racing too fast to remember anything at all.

A marketing professor, maybe 10 years older than me, walked into the conference room. Geoff was dressed in what I remember as "summer academic casual" (polo shirt and shorts), and he sat across from me. Geoff placed a file folder down on the table and started - STARTED! - our conversation by saying this, and I quote: "Dave, I looked at your resume and you have taken some bad advice."

Hah! You are wrong, sir! I have not taken ANY advice!

That was not really my reply. Instead, I said "I take responsibility for everything I've done."

Geoff chuckled and said, "Good answer, Dave." What a way to start. And actually, I had taken some advice. Not enough of the good kind, too much of the bad kind, and far too little of the kind that could help me keep my job. That's why I was there.

Wow, interviewing can be hard! I don't remember anything else from that day. I really don't. And they hired me.

From Bitter to Better

The Chicagoland days were over and even though I had managed to land my next job, it was only temporary and I was bitter. I was angry at myself for not succeeding at Chicagoland, especially since all my colleagues did. I still check the department's website from time to time and they're all still there, two-thirds of the three-headed mentoring monster (Willie passed away several years ago) and almost all the people hired around the time I was hired. Now they are tenured and secure roughly 20 years later, except those who have moved on from Chicagoland to take administrative positions elsewhere. I was also angry at the whole lot of them for not taking better care of me. Whose idea was it to change direction, from teaching to research, without telling the new hires? And who came up with that ridiculous three-headed mentoring monster idea, anyway? And how did I end up with three guys who didn't seem to care very much about my success? And why couldn't I figure any of this out when I was there? As summer turned to fall and city traffic was replaced with country scenery, I was still thinking about these things. My time and energy needed to be moved in a more productive direction: preparing for a lot of sections of MKTG 325 Buyer Behavior, the only course that I would teach.

This was more teaching all at one time than I was used to. One of the good things about my six years at Chicagoland, along with my years at Michigan, is that I had the opportunity to teach a lot of different courses to undergrads and MBA students (introduction to marketing, advertising, business-to-business marketing, sales, integrated marketing communications, marketing strategy, marketing research), so the focus on just this one course was fine with me. If I could plan my work better and stay on top of things, this would give me more time to figure out how to do my research. This was important to me. I felt like

David Aron

I had to come through for Keith and write something worthy of his journal, to build upon whatever momentum I had in the hyper-narrow niche of consumer grudgeholding behavior, the topic of my first paper.

At NIU, I had my new office, smaller than my last one. A little cabinet instead of a full wall of bookshelves. A view of a pond and trees instead of staring into the windows of another building across the street. More balance in the numbers of women and men, compared to the mostly male make-up of Chicagoland's marketing faculty. The fact that I was at NIU only to teach made me feel a bit like an outsider among these researchers. At Chicagoland, I was expected to teach, conduct and publish research, and participate in committees in the marketing department, in the business school, and for the university. A mentor might have helped give me perspective beyond just doing those things. At Northern and not on the tenure track, teaching was all they asked of me. But the problem was that if I ever wanted to pursue tenure again, whether at NIU or some other university, I simply could not focus only on teaching. I was in a bind: No matter how well I performed in the classroom, if I could not show I was also capable of creating publishable academic research, I would not find another tenure track job. This was a new start, but a familiar dilemma.

This challenge spurred a new attitude within me: say "yes" to everything, even without prompting. At Chicagoland, well-intentioned advice from a senior professor urged junior faculty to "keep your head down and stay out of trouble." This misplaced mentoring, a topic for chapter 8, proved counterproductive. Such advice, to play it safe, simply led to me going unnoticed. This was a formula for irrelevance at that institution. I wouldn't let it happen again. To become more visible and desirable as a collaborator, I promised myself to actively seek out meetings and volunteer for committees that would get me noticed. I wanted to become someone that others wanted to work with.

The Intervention

A week into fall semester, my first semester at Northern, everything changed. I was sitting in my office, having just finished one of my classes and preparing for the next one. Geoff, the guy who interviewed me, and now my new senior colleague, walked into my office unannounced. "Let's get lunch." With a nod of his head, beckoning me toward the door, he turned around and walked back out. This was not a question, it was a statement. It was a lifeline. We drove to a nearby sandwich shop. Joining us was Tim, whom I had only met briefly by that time. Geoff and Tim had worked together at Northern for a long time. They knew each other well, knew each other's families, the names of their children, along with the families of my other new colleagues. They talked about their weekend plans. They asked about my family, my children. This camaraderie, this affection, was so different compared to Chicagoland.

Tim looked at me from across the table. "Dave, why don't you tell us about your research," he asked. That was unexpected. *What do they care about my research?* They either hired me despite my research productivity, or, given the job description, with little regard for my research. *You brought me here to teach, right?*

So I described my one research paper, which was on the concept of consumers who hold grudges against the stores and companies that have led to negative outcomes and experiences. This was kind of an offshoot of my dissertation, which was entitled *Consumer Regret.* As you surely have guessed, that was about consumers who regret the purchases they made. It happens to all of us! After I defended my dissertation and started at Chicagoland, I just seemed to hit a research wall. It was hard for me to collect data, in order to build upon my dissertation for future research as many new grad students do. Regret involves blaming oneself for an outcome, and apparently I just wasn't very good at getting people to share stories of things they blamed themselves for.

The frustration grew, and I was not a productive researcher or writer in the months after I defended. Then I had kind of a revelation, a big idea. I decided to flip the script, and write not about consumer regret (you blame yourself for your bad consumer outcome) but about consumer grudgeholding (you blame someone else for your bad consumer outcome). People don't seem to mind talking about their grudges, about blaming somebody or something else. There were really almost no existing academic marketing research papers on consumer regret, often called "buyer's remorse" which might explain why at that time - in Google's infancy and before AI was widely available - I could find so little information about what I was calling regret. And there were just a few papers about consumer grudgeholding, most often written by Keith and his colleagues, published in his journal. Those served as the springboard for my paper, too little and too late for the folks at Chicagoland but, curiously, of some interest to my new colleagues at Northern. And if you are wondering if all this talk about deep-dive research on regret and holding grudges is just me, projecting my own feelings through my work, then I guess that makes two of us.

After I finished talking about my paper, Geoff shared his thoughts. "You've got some good ideas but you don't seem to know what to do with them. We're here to sit down with you and figure things out. Let's see what we can do together." This outreach, this extension of a helping hand, this continuation of the compassion Keith had shared, how could I have been so blind, so ignorant to have missed this kind of mentoring over the previous 17 years at Eastland, at TechFirm, at Michigan, and at Chicagoland (that's regret) or was that kind of mentoring simply not there, selfishly withheld from me (and that's grudgeholding)?

I'm also including this again to prove a point. This was no less than a career-saving, life-altering mentoring intervention by Geoff and Tim. I was not a tenure-track junior colleague at NIU. My success would not add much if anything to the aggregate success of their marketing department. My productivity would not even spare them the energy and expense of conducting another job search to replace me. I was on a nine month contract, they barely knew me and then I was going to vanish, gone to my next job in a few months. But Geoff and Tim were ready to work with me. And that is exactly what we did.

Transcending Transactions

If you are reading this as a mentee or somebody seeking a mentor, this is something so important to keep in mind. Mentors have reasons for doing what they do that transcend transactions. Even while it's true many mentors offer their services without financial compensation, there are several compelling reasons why individuals choose to share their wisdom with those in need:

- **Personal Satisfaction:** Many people find intrinsic reward in helping others grow and develop.

- **Giving Back:** Some mentors feel a sense of obligation to share their knowledge and experience with the next generation.
- **Networking Opportunities:** Building relationships with mentees can lead to a whole new set of professional and personal connections.
- **Staying Engaged:** Mentoring can help mentors stay connected to the latest news in their field and continue learning.
- **Career Development:** In some cases, mentoring can be a requirement or benefit for career advancement.
- **Corporate Social Responsibility:** Organizations may encourage employees to mentor as part of their CSR initiatives.

Why did Geoff and Tim decide to offer this mentoring intervention? I was afraid to ask at that time. In the ensuing years, long after I left NIU, I continued to work with both Geoff and Tim, and I asked them (separately) why they devoted so much time to my cause. They would talk about my interesting research topic, grudgeholding, but offer little more than that. Just a couple of humble, helpful guys, I guess.

By the time our visit to the sub shop ended, Geoff and Tim thoroughly blew my mind and had found themselves in me a devoted fan and protégé. Geoff organized a meeting for the following week that included him, Tim, and two junior colleagues, Kim and Sandy. That was the first of many meetings we had, all focused on my research. Kim, on the tenure track at NIU, was an integral part of our new project team, even though my research would pale in comparison to her own prolific research productivity. Sandy was a marketing instructor at NIU, not on the tenure track, but she hoped to pursue her PhD in the future. Geoff and Tim invited her to join us, to see how she enjoyed the research process. Kind of a test drive.

Geoff ran our meetings while I listened and learned. He divided the work among us, and kept our team on track. Tim, who could count being an amazing networker among his superpowers, shared some of our ideas with the many journal editors he knew, looking for ideal opportunities to publish this still-unique research topic of consumer grudgeholding. And I shared my deeper knowledge of this little corner of the marketing research world. Geoff split up the work among us and we all wrote. I edited, and Tim sent the papers in for review to the editors he knew. This approach worked. And the results? The results were kind of amazing!

Keep in mind this was academic research, so I'm not talking about amazing in terms of revenue or profitability. I'm talking about productivity, about publishing articles. In my six years at Chicagoland, I published one article. In my one year at Northern, I published or made substantial progress on five articles. They weren't all published in my one year at NIU, but all five were published within two years as a result of our collaboration. Five articles in that time, versus one in six years. Five articles in five different journals (including one in Keith's *Journal of Consumer Satisfaction, Dissatisfaction, and Complaining Behavior*). Northern versus Chicagoland. Alone versus a team. Old Dave versus New Dave. The impact of caring mentors.

This is how I see what I've been calling this mentoring intervention, my Mentorvention. My collaborations with these two tenured professors changed my entire career trajectory. Like Keith, my new colleagues had had little to gain... professionally, anyway... by lifting me up and working with me.

But they did anyway. That one-year position led to my next job, one I've held for almost 20 years as of this writing. Keith showed me what professional, personal, and passionate guidance looked like. He was the first real mentor to me, when I needed one most. Once again, it's that old line about when the student is ready… or when the junior faculty member is desperate… the teacher will come. Keith's influence, as well as that of Geoff and Tim at Northern Illinois University, saved my academic career. As a researcher, as a teacher, as a member of a university faculty, as a mentor, and as an empathetic member of this, my chosen community, I owe it all to Keith, Geoff, and Tim.

Bad News, Good News, Better News

As the school year marched on, many of the administrative issues involved in running a department, events I had been shielded from at Chicagoland, were now happening right in front of me and having an impact on my career. This time, I paid attention. Denise, who was Chair of Northern's Marketing faculty when she hired me, was promoted to Dean of the entire business school, and Geoff was a popular choice to take her place as Chair. Aware of this, I let him know I hoped he would remember my hard work and research productivity when it came time to fill the position I had been holding down for the past several months.

Geoff had some news for me. He told me he admired how I was turning my career in the right direction, but there was something important for me to understand: it would not be enough. Despite the great success I was experiencing, writing and publishing with my team, the journals I was publishing in were not selective enough, not prestigious enough, to guarantee anything. This improvement was a step in the right direction but was still below the research standards of the department. I was disappointed but accepted this news. I understood. This entire experience was a gift. The research I finally learned how to do was so much more than I expected in this year of getting back on my feet. This was the year of my Mentorvention, and I wanted nothing more than to show Geoff and Tim that their efforts would continue to pay off. I wanted to stay at NIU and I wanted to earn my way back onto the tenure track.

It was around this time I sat in on a marketing faculty meeting. As a visiting professor, this would have been an easy one to skip. But I was still in "say yes to everything" mode at Northern, and I wanted to show my commitment to the department and the people around me. I was sitting next to another senior faculty member named Mick. Mick, roughly the same age as Geoff and Tim, was one of the happiest faculty members I had ever worked with, a sales management professor who lit up the room and would have been a marvelous salesman to buy from.

As the meeting ended, those in attendance were given the option to leave or stay if interested in the next discussion: that of attending the next jobs conference (remember those?) to interview the next crop of new and rising PhDs for the next year's new faculty hires. *They're going to talk about my job!* Many people stood up to leave, a few others went to refresh their coffee, and those still in their chairs took advantage of this short break to exchange small talk. During this noisy transition, I leaned over to Mick and whispered, "Do you think I can stay for this part?"

Mick's voice cut through the commotion and filled the room. "Hell, yes!"

Those words still warm my heart. I felt wanted. I felt more than ever that I belonged. Maybe I could stay at this place, despite Geoff's warnings.

No such luck. Before long, Geoff let me know he decided not to pursue the Chair position at that time. Another senior colleague, Tanujah, became the new marketing department chair, replacing Denise. Tanujah was an international marketing professor, with an office right next to mine and we got along well. Shortly after her promotion was announced, I raised the topic of staying at Northern with her. She was direct, echoing Geoff's earlier words about the journals I was publishing in. She continued, telling me that since she was going to be teaching fewer classes in her new leadership role, she wanted to switch the department's jobs conference focus toward finding somebody new who could teach international marketing, not consumer behavior. "You're welcome to apply," she told me, but politely urged me to keep this new information in mind.

Okay, I get it. One, my research, while growing, was still below this department's standard. Two, my research and teaching specialty, consumer behavior, was no longer what the department needed. I'm picking up some clues here. My time at Northern Illinois University was coming to an end. But what a year. The most important year of my career.

Meanwhile, you should know there was another side to this. As much as I loved my time at Northern, I was not just sitting around hoping to get lucky a second time. Among the schools I had applied to during my final year at Chicagoland was a small private school outside of Chicago called Dominican University. Smaller than Chicagoland. Much smaller than Northern. Much, much smaller than Michigan. Tiny, in a good way. This was a university where marketing and all the business school departments were combined into one. At this school, there weren't twenty-some marketing professors like at Chicagoland and Northern, there were two. Neither of them was me; I didn't get the job, obviously, which is why I ended up at Northern.

Chapter 7: Mentoring Intervention

Specifically, the marketing faculty consisted of one senior member named Al and now a younger guy, hired instead of me, named Michael. I applied for the job Michael ended up getting. During this process, I made it to the campus interview stage, so I got to visit the school and meet some of the other faculty members.

At academic interviews, the applicant will generally meet a lot of people, teach a course, and present their research. At that time, though, Dominican was so overwhelmingly focused on teaching that there was no research presentation required for me at all. And now here at NIU, I was doing a lot of research! But no matter. During my visit, I taught a marketing class to their students and had some great conversations with the other members of the business school in this very new environment. During one of these meetings, Al let me know he taught marketing, international marketing, international business, marketing research, consumer behavior... whatever they needed. This was different too. At Michigan, to earn a few bucks while in school I taught whatever they let me teach but the full-time faculty members generally focused on one topic or two. That way they could spend more time on their research. And as I would find out at Northern, if your teaching or research specialty is already fulfilled by others in the department, you might not be the right fit.

When I asked Al which teaching specialty they were seeking, he said, "All of them. We teach everything here." I got along so well with Al, but I did not get the position. Alas, Dominican was among the several schools that did not hire me. However, Al and I stayed in touch during my year at NIU. See? I was learning! Just pick up the phone! Al even invited me to visit as a guest lecturer for his classes while I was working at Northern. Note this as another example of what a mentee can offer to a mentor! It was Dominican's rejection that led me to DeKalb, to Geoff, and Tim. An unfortunate outcome that turned into the best opportunity I could ever wish for.

Striking While the Irony is Hot

While I was at Northern, working with Geoff, Tim, and the others in hopes of rebuilding my career and hoping to stay at NIU, I knew my contract would expire soon and so I continued to keep my eyes open for opportunities at other local schools. And again, relatively late in the jobs conference-centered hiring cycle, and to my amazement, Al's school, little Dominican University, once again advertised they were looking for a marketing professor! What? Again? Were they expanding that marketing group, growing from two to three? Or was Michael not working out? That would be odd: Chicagoland gave me six years before pointing me toward the door, and even a high-pressure research powerhouse like Michigan gave their people at least three years. But one year? The transition from a hard-core research program (which describes most schools that have doctoral programs) to a small teaching school like Dominican can be difficult. Maybe the new guy couldn't adapt, I guessed.

So I applied again. This time, I was something of a known quantity thanks to the relationship I maintained with Al. And this time, I got it! I got the job at Dominican. I'm back on the tenure track! And now, here comes a surprise: Thanks to my months with Geoff and Tim, my research productivity was suddenly, relatively... impressive! At least to the folks at Dominican, if not Northern. If that isn't ironic enough, Dominican's business school Dean would soon ask me to take the lead in preparing my colleagues for my new school's transition into a (again, relatively speaking) more research-focused department. And I would get to work next to my newest mentor, Al. This seemed too good to be true. And it was. In another ironic twist, the reason Dominican was seeking another marketing professor so soon after hiring Michael is that Al was the one leaving, moving to a different university. Michael was staying and Al was the person I would replace as I moved on to my next opportunity. Ready for one more ironic development? As it turns out, I was asked to take over Al's courses, including International Marketing. That might be amusing only to me, and I never told Tanujah. So even though I would once again be the new player on the team, I now had quite a few years of experience under my belt, as well as the career-altering lessons I learned at Northern. Another transition, another brand new environment. But now, I had to transform from the mentee to the mentor.

Chapter 8: The Mentoring Hydra

My months at Northern were a gift, and my relationship with Geoff and Tim counted as the luckiest break, professionally speaking, anyone could hope for. I must say too that if it weren't for Keith's generosity a year before that, I might not have had the courage to step out of my comfort zone and accept the mentoring intervention my two colleagues at NIU offered. I can absolutely imagine myself saying "no thanks" to Geoff that day he asked me to lunch. That lunch meeting blasted me way out of my comfort zone and if I had said "no," I never would have realized how safe I truly was. What a mistake that would have been. And of course, my pairing with Sandeep several years earlier, before I knew Keith or Geoff or Tim or even what my career path would look like, was pretty random and of great benefit as well. Let's face it, everything I've experienced, good and bad, back and forth, up and down, zigging and zagging, led me to the happy place I'm at today. Good mentors help you find and keep control of your career, as coaches, teachers, confidants, advisors, and cheerleaders, formal and informal, all stretching and redefining the meaning of the word mentor in their own way.

And then… there are the others. From the three-headed mentoring misery at Chicagoland, to others I have encountered during my career journey, there have been a number of people that got in my way, threw up roadblocks, and otherwise slowed my progress. Of course at the time it feels like these actions are intentional. But it's very possible they are not intentional at all. An important lesson here is not to take every slight as a personal attack. Like with Mandy. I don't count Mandy as a mentor in any way, even though her pal Ronnie, my boss's boss, might count as a missed opportunity. One of my many lingering, cringe-inducing memories of Mandy was her wedding. No, of course I wasn't invited to her wedding. And of course I wouldn't go, even if she invited everybody from our department to travel out to New York to participate in her nuptials and even if she offered to help cover some of our travel expenses. And, as a matter of fact, that's exactly what she did.

As I write this, I'm trying very hard not to sound whiny. I think you have a sense of my relationship with Mandy by this point. But Mandy did indeed invite everybody in our Electronic Shopper group (Arnold, our manager, Tom and two other sales reps, three account support reps, and our office manager). Everyone except for me. She made a point during one of her visits to Columbus, at a department meeting, to bring up the latest news about her upcoming wedding and reception. She called out every person in the room, by name, one by one, to check on their attendance plans, except for one person. Yes, literally, I was the only person in the department not invited. Objectively speaking, her bringing up her wedding in the meeting was unprofessional (though, I guess, a fairly efficient use of her time in Columbus). Subjectively speaking, who would even do something like that? Well, Mandy did. This goes back to my point that I don't think this was a direct stab at me. It was more like I didn't matter to Mandy. She was just the star of her own story, just like you are the star of yours and I'm the star of mine. In her story, I was just a non-essential character.

But back to the mentors. Whether it's a formal mentoring program or an informal relationship you have with a mentor, these relationships can go wrong for any number of reasons. In this chapter, let's look at what I'll call the Mentoring Hydra. The Hydra is a monster from Greek mythology, a symbol of our struggle against insurmountable challenges. Battling the Hydra symbolizes the value of persistence, strategy, and collaboration in the face of danger and adversity. The Hydra is a nine-headed, snake-like monster, and to stay true to this illustration, I will share nine examples of the kinds of mentors you, too, may have to overcome through persistence, strategy, and collaboration. These are people you would do better to avoid if you can, to steer clear of if possible. And, if necessary, to break away from in order to keep your hands on the wheel of your career.

The Missing Mentors

Let's start with a group I'll call The Missing Mentors. These relationships are the most benign of the otherwise disappointing relationships, but they can still hurt. It's hard to say a mentoring relationship even existed at all because it vanished so quickly.

Here's one example of a missing mentor. When I was exploring different marketing doctoral programs, the journey that led me to the University of Michigan, I spent some time looking up different university marketing professors whose work interested me. I reached out to one such professor at Northwestern University named Gale, hoping I could set up a meeting with him on campus. Now in my current position we don't have a PhD program in business, so I don't meet a lot of doctoral students. Every once in a while, one of my advisees or students will let me know they are thinking of continuing their education, and so I get very excited when I do meet somebody who hopes to pursue their doctorate. I become a firehose of questions and advice. This has happened four or five times since I've been at Dominican.

In contrast, I would imagine at a powerhouse research-focused marketing department like Northwestern's, there is not any novelty in meeting a prospective PhD, and the professors work with doctoral students on a daily basis. Gale, however, seemed very interested in talking to me about my background at TechFirm (pretty high-tech online retail at the time) and about his research. Gale and I had a few phone calls together, and I could really feel a relationship starting to grow. I set up a date to drive out and meet him, coincidentally, at the school where I earned my bachelor's degree. When I arrived on campus, I walked into the marketing faculty office and asked the receptionist to let Gale know I was there for our meeting. She looked at me as if I were speaking another language. "He knows I'm going to meet him at 10," I added.

"Are you one of his students?" she asked.

"Not yet, but maybe soon. I'm thinking about applying to your doctoral program.

"Oh. We don't set up appointments for our faculty to meet prospective applicants."

That doesn't seem like very good marketing to me!

"But he knows I'm coming," I said. "We set up a time."

"I'm sorry but I'll see if one of his graduate assistants is available."

Gale, where did you go? How could you forget? We hit it off so well on the phone last week!

Do you remember how on those old fashioned desk phones you could have your thumb on the hang-up button while you pretend to dial a number with your other fingers? I'm pretty sure that's

Chapter 8: The Mentoring Hydra

what the receptionist did. Faking a phone call back in the day required more effort than it does now! I drove all this way out to connect with a possible mentor and I couldn't believe how I was being treated, by Gale and by the department gatekeeper.

I sat down to wait. A moment later two young men, looking like they were in their mid- to late-twenties, walked up to the receptionist's desk. Maybe these are Gale's doctoral students? Are these my guys? As they spoke to her, I stood up to meet them. They quickly turned from her desk and walked back toward the door as if to leave, walking right past me. I caught up to them.

"Are you guys doctoral students here?" I asked.

They nodded.

"Can I ask you a couple of quick questions?"

One of them replied, "Sure."

I told them I was supposed to meet Gale and one of the two said that Gale could be really hard to find. Oh great. I had a whole bunch of questions for Gale, written on a notepad, expecting to chat over coffee that morning. I wasn't really ready to go off script like this. I asked the first question that popped into my head.

"Do you do a lot of work with other departments, like the Psychology Department?" This was on my mind because Gale's research was in consumer behavior… applied psychology… and that's what I was interested in. By the way, I was a psychology major as an undergrad, at the very school I was now visiting.

The grad students looked at each other. One frowned and shook his head and the other replied. "No. They don't know anything we don't know."

That's not what I expected to hear. I guess I don't really know what I expected to hear. I know I didn't care for the answer or the condescending manner in which it was stated. That's MY major you're talking about, pal! That was the end of my visit. I left to go home.

As it turns out, I finished my application and I did get accepted to that program. After that visit, though, I had no intention of going. Who knows if Gale would have even been a mentor to me? My experience with Gale definitely fits in among the archetypes of the missing mentor.

1. Gale the Ghost:

Even if the details were not the same, have you experienced anything like the story I just shared? One where it sure seemed like your relationship with your version of Gale was going to be a good one. You really hit it off at your first meeting… and then that was it. Maybe Gale left the job or just ran out of time for you. But as far as you can tell, Gale is gone, disappeared, and not returning your messages and nowhere to be found.

2. Willie the Unwilling:

Willie the Unwilling might have been assigned to you from up above, from corporate or HR, and obligated to participate as part of a formal mentoring program that seemed like a good idea at the time. Willie is really someone who doesn't want to be part of the program, seeing mentorship as an unwelcome interruption to their regular duties or routine. If you can find Willie, they might give you advice or answer your questions. But given a choice, they wouldn't even be part of the plan. Their disengagement is palpable, and their advice may just feel empty or insincere. While they might provide basic information when pressed, their lack of enthusiasm and genuine interest can be discouraging for a mentee. It's essential to recognize these signs early on and to seek guidance from other sources to avoid wasting valuable time and energy. They'd be happy if you just kept walking.

3. Whit the Uninterested:

Whit the Uninterested might hold a position of authority, perhaps even as a direct supervisor. Whit is someone who views mentoring as an extracurricular activity rather than a core responsibility. Whit might be in a position to offer some strong insight or wisdom and might even be your boss. But Whit really doesn't see mentoring as part of their job description. Their focus remains firmly on their own role and deliverables, with little to no room for nurturing the professional growth of others. While they may possess valuable knowledge and experience, their disinterest can create a barrier to meaningful mentorship. A classic example is the mentor who dismisses a mentee's questions with a curt, "That's not my job." Such interactions can be demoralizing and hinder professional development. Whit is the supervisor, and you are the supervised. To them, that's enough. Get back to work.

Managing the Missing Mentors: Finding the Support You Need

In my conversations with my former students and advisees, I hear many examples of missing mentors and ghost mentors. One meeting and then no contact. Or contact that offers so little in terms of learning and growth. Your hopes rising, your imagination sparking, only to vanish when emails are ignored and calls are not returned. If these relationships are part of an informal program, you might just walk away. Why keep yelling into an empty space? Instead, seek out someone else, another mentor, a new relationship. Be sure to articulate your hopes for the relationship, and importantly, discover theirs as well. What can you offer them? Be aware of and respectful toward their time constraints. And remember to set a firm date for the next meeting or conversation... or set up regularly scheduled encounters.

However, if these mismatches are part of a formal program at work or with an organization, then tread more carefully. Here is where reputations can be made or damaged. It's likely that Willie the Unwilling, Whit the Uninterested, and Gale the Ghost are senior to you and higher up in the org chart. There might even be repercussions if their bosses learn not everybody is playing by their rules... for the mentors and, indirectly, for you. You definitely do not want a mentor to turn into your nemesis (which can happen... keep reading!) You might go back to the mentor and discuss specific projects common to both of your goals and needs. You can go to the organizer of the program and ask for another mentor, to gain alternate perspectives on the issues you are dealing with without throwing shade at anybody else. You can even establish informal mentoring relationships on your own, with people who are more willing to help guide you

The Mismatched Mentors

Three more heads of the mentoring Hydra can be labeled as Mismatched Mentors. These kinds of relationships can be more dangerous to you than the Missing Mentors. With Mismatched

Chapter 8: The Mentoring Hydra

Mentors, you might find yourself in situations where you have a mentor with the best of intentions, but who still ends up doing harm to your career in some way, often due to your own lack of experience and judgment, or their blind spots, biases, or misaligned backgrounds.

One example of a mentoring mismatch might manifest through advice that turns out poorly for you. Have you ever been told to "keep your head down" in your work environment? This is the kind of well-meaning warning we hear all the time. Be seen and not heard. Don't jump into any situation that doesn't concern you. Well, why? Why hide my head? So nobody knows I'm there? So I won't get credit for my contributions? So I can't stake claim to my role in strengthening my team? I will admit there is wisdom in not inserting yourself into volatile situations, as long as you are not sacrificing your ability to have ideas, your right to have an opinion, and your responsibility to advocate for yourself.

The second example is more specific. You might have noticed from what you've read so far that I enjoy a little wordplay, I admire alliteration, and I've never met a pun I didn't like. Along those lines, when it comes time to put a title to the papers and presentations I'm developing, ideas like this emerge:

- Planning for the Apes: Coping with Guerrilla Consumer Behavior when the Courts Won't Help.
- Venn Push Comes to Shove: Toward Understanding Dysfunctional Consumer Behavior.
- Let Me Eat Cake!: Survival Tips for your First Study Abroad Program.
- Student, Sing Your Song: The CHIRP Program.
- Half-classed and Partially Flipped: Teaching a Crowded Seminar Course.

- Futility Theory: Consumer Valuation of Privacy in Exchange for Convenience.

And my favorite, which simply has not received the appreciation it deserves:

- We, Inventing the Real: Approaches to Developing a College Course on Consumer Satisfaction.

Well, some people did not appreciate my attempts at humor. I would receive comments from colleagues suggesting such wordplay is inappropriate. It was beneath my standing, not suited for the profession. It does not "fit in." I would not be taken seriously. While I'm pretty sure my critics' collective hearts were in the right places, my thoughts on this come from a marketing perspective: I want to entice people to read what I'm writing. And, especially while at Chicagoland University, I wanted… I needed… to find as much fun as possible in my otherwise dismal workplace. Fun fact: all those titles listed above did become published papers or conference presentations. Here are some more examples of mismatched mentors who likely would have preferred those titles never saw the light of day:

4. Wes the Well-Intentioned:

Your prospective mentor, whether formally or informally paired with you, might be an expert in one area (theirs) but not as much in another (yours). That kind of mismatch can take on other forms too, such as when the advice shared by your mentor might have been appropriate when they were just starting out, but is outdated now. Or it might fit their style without taking into account your own unique superpowers. Mentors like Wes the Well-Intentioned might mean well but still provide misguided advice that can harm or slow your development. As you just read above, I have had examples of Wes that seemed well-intentioned at the time but proved to be, in retrospect, bad. Advice like this might force you to take your hands off the wheel and cede control over your career.

5. Alex the All-Knowing:

Alex might seem like an ideal mentor. When I say "all-knowing," I mean it in a positive sense: Alex can be an incredible resource when it comes to your job, your environment, you name it. However, there's a risk that, in trying to help you and others, Alex might become stretched too thin, inadvertently limiting the support they can offer. It's a reality that when someone has a lot to offer, many people will seek to benefit from their expertise, just as you do.

In my experience, I realized Alex had a lot on their plate, managing responsibilities across various projects and teams. While this was a testament to Alex's abilities, it also meant I sometimes questioned whether I was learning to navigate workplace challenges on my own. Alex took care of many aspects of our work together, which was incredibly helpful. However, I wonder if this also affected my sense of agency, as I didn't have to face certain challenges others might have had to handle independently or through my own leadership.

In contrast, remember the episode with the unhappy letter-writing student while I was still at Chicagoland? In that case, Phil expected me to come up with ideas on my own. To take ownership. While working with Alex can ultimately lead to a positive experience, it's worth noting that over-reliance on someone like Alex the All-Knowing could lead to a dependency that might limit personal growth. If your first instinct is always to go to Alex for help, you might miss opportunities to develop your own problem-solving skills.

There is another, more extreme version of Alex the All-Knowing. You might encounter a mentor like Alex who despite their brilliance and expertise, is less approachable. This type of Alex might have a wealth of knowledge, but little patience for questions and intolerant of mistakes. Your relationship with your mentor would be damaged if you are too intimidated to seek guidance from them.

6. Tracy the Transactor:

There was one member of my three-headed mentoring mistake at Chicagoland I actually got along with quite well. I found him to be inspiring and fun to work with, and he seemed to take a personal interest in me. I can take much of the responsibility for not pursuing a deeper relationship with Tracy, or for not asking more questions. One reason for this is that Tracy had a habit of concluding our conversations by asking me, "Do you have any idea how much I charge for this kind of advice?" No, I do not. Is that a rhetorical question or am I supposed to answer? Probably rhetorical, just in case I didn't express how much I valued Tracy's ideas.

In the last chapter, I wrote about my time at Northern, after leaving Chicagoland, and about the time and energy that Geoff and Tim devoted to me. There was never the slightest suggestion of payment or reciprocity of any kind. There are reasons mentors do what they do, which includes personal satisfaction, the desire to give back, hope of creating networking opportunities, wanting to stay engaged, and the intention of further developing their own career. Mentors might even receive some sort of tangible reward for their efforts, perhaps as part of their service to their organization. There are people who get paid to coach, to teach, and to train, and their contributions to your career have a great deal of overlap with what your mentor can offer you. But you don't pay a mentor. So stop bringing that up, Tracy. It suggests you view mentoring as a transaction, an exchange. It also tells me you are lacking genuine care for my development.

Managing the Mismatched Mentors: Awareness and Engagement

These archetypes of mismatched mentors might seem more diverse than the examples I shared of missing mentors, but they have a common thread. In each of these cases, the mentors are not trying to avoid you or do any harm, it's just that you must manage the relationships with a blend of awareness and strategic engagement. With a mentor like Wes the Well-Intentioned, it's important to carefully evaluate the advice you receive, considering whether it aligns with your current context and personal style. Seeking input from diverse sources can help you make more informed decisions while ensuring you maintain control over your career. Similarly, working with an Alex the All-Knowing mentor can be incredibly beneficial, but it's crucial to develop self-reliance and set boundaries to avoid over-dependence. By taking ownership of your learning and tackling challenges independently, you can grow into a more confident and capable professional.

On the other hand, dealing with mentors like Tracy the Transactor requires a more nuanced approach. With Tracy, it's vital to clarify expectations and ensure the relationship is built on mutual respect rather than transactions. Does Tracy not think they're benefiting from this relationship too? Are they too focused on lamenting their lack of monetary gain? Prioritize genuine connections with mentors who truly care about your development. This will help you achieve long-term success, allowing you to benefit from their guidance without feeling undervalued or compromised. In all cases, focus on making the most of your interactions by being well-prepared, while also seeking support from more approachable mentors to balance the dynamic.

The Malignant Mentors

Three more heads of the mentoring Hydra can be labeled as Malignant. These relationships might start as beneficial, and the mentors start as supportive to you and your career. However, the malignant mentors can become toxic and destructive. These people are not as benign as the missing mentors, and not nearly as manageable as the mismatched mentors. Relationships with malignant mentors can be destructive, leading not only to loss of control over your career, but can also cause damage to your reputation, crushing your self-confidence, and possibly even costing you your job. The damage might come from their personal attacks or vendettas, or simply because they are standing in your path. Either way, malignant mentors do exist and must be handled with care and skill.

Let me share an example to support this point. One day when I was still at Eastland I was at lunch with my boss Whit along with Harry, our security director at the Mall. We were in a booth at the Olive Garden restaurant right outside our parking lot, and whenever we went there for lunch we would share a salad, and these two grown men would engage in a hot pepper eating contest. I, also a grown man, would enjoy the rest of the salad and simply observe their attempted Alpha behavior. During this particular lunch, in between hot peppers swallowed whole by those two adult men, our conversation turned to Harry's second-in-command, a mall security officer named Charlie. Whit wondered aloud if Charlie would be a good fit as security director at one of our nearby malls. Harry said, matter-of-factly, that Charlie is gaining experience but wasn't quite ready to be promoted yet. Whit asked me my opinion, and I replied that Charlie seemed like a great colleague, a take-charge guy who really knew what he was doing. Definitely worth consideration for the vacant role.

With that, and almost certainly as a result of all the hot peppers he had just eaten, Whit excused himself to use the bathroom. Once Whit was out of sight, Harry casually reached across the table, grabbed me by the tie, and pulled me up to his face. Nose-to-nose, he hissed "Hey, how about you shut your mouth and mind your own business?" Ooh, that breath! I pushed Harry away and stage-whispered back that since Whit asked me, this was my business. Harry stood up, laughing. He walked to my side of the booth, sat down where Whit had been sitting and put his arm around me… just a couple of big boys horsing around, everybody! Nothing to see here! Enjoy your breadsticks. Harry leaned into my ear: "You think it's easy to find a good Number Two? It isn't! I'm not going to give up Charlie."

Whit returned, his heartburn surely further warmed by seeing his employees bonding in that way. We went back to the mall where, unsurprisingly, Whit and Harry spent the rest of the afternoon in their respective offices with their doors closed. And Charlie wasn't going anywhere. Until that day I thought Harry was a good leader and in some situations he might have fit that description. But a real leader is focused on creating more leaders, not hoarding them and stunting their careers. These are the types of malignant mentors:

7. Harry the Hoarder:

Harry was just one example I've seen of a boss and would-be mentor that puts their own needs above those of their protégés and their department or company overall. Someone like Harry, who prevents the advancement of others for their own benefit, clearly diminishes opportunities for mentees, and those opportunities might be rare. Another example of Harry the Hoarder can be seen in Rodney, the third head of my three-headed mentoring monster at Chicagoland. Along with Willie, my passive, missing mentor, and Tracy, my message-missing mismatched mentor, Rodney's influence was more malignant. He seemed to be primarily motivated by personal gain, prioritizing his needs over his mentees'. Rodney would be glad to work with you if you would do his work for him or share your data with him. Otherwise he had no time for you.

8. Lori the Loyalist:

Recall the story of Lori the Loyalist. When I asked her if she thought it would be okay if I missed an abruptly called meeting the next morning, she betrayed my confidence and told our boss, and our boss was quite unhappy. I was even accused of dereliction of my responsibility. In the story of Lori the Loyalist, it's crucial to understand the dynamics at play when you have a mentor in the workplace. While mentors can provide guidance and support, it's important to remember their primary loyalty lies with the organization employing them. This doesn't mean they can't or won't help you grow, but it does mean their advice and actions may be influenced by their own career interests and obligations to the company.

Take, for example, the experience I had with Geoff and Tim, who were true allies and demonstrated a willingness to support me well beyond the typical boundaries of our professional roles. True, they were tenured and safe in their jobs, but there was no formally prescribed reason for them to help me like they did. In fact, many people would use that status and position as reasons

NOT to be helpful. Instead, Geoff and Tim showed me that not all colleagues are solely focused on their survival within the company. However, my experience with Lori highlighted the opposite end of the spectrum. When she disclosed what I thought was private information to our boss, it was a stark reminder that while not everyone in the workplace is your rival or enemy, they still might not have your best interests at heart. Lori's actions led to my supervisor questioning my suitability for my job, which could have had severe consequences for my career. It sure didn't help.

9. Noel the Controller:

In the world of mentorship, there's a dark side where power dynamics can spiral out of control, creating an environment that is not only unsupportive but downright harmful. In contrast to Alex the All-Knowing, Noel the Controller embodies the worst-case scenario of a mentor who abuses their authority and positions themselves as a gatekeeper to power. One example of Noel was a professor at Michigan who would use intimidation and threats of failure to force himself onto PhD. student committees, commandeering them and refusing to step aside. Noel would insert themself into every aspect of a student-mentee's development. This kind of mentor thrives on controlling every decision, making it clear any attempt to remove them from their position would result in severe consequences. The fear they instill hinders the mentee's autonomy and creates a toxic environment where the mentee feels trapped rather than supported. Mentors like Noel the Controller exist throughout different industries and firms.

Adding to this mix is the demeaning behavior I witnessed from another extreme version of Noel, this time as a C-suite executive at TechFirm. This occurred shortly after Jim left

TechFirm, still early in my time at the company. Noel, appropriately, wanted to meet with Jim's team to better understand the steps needed to be taken from above. During my meeting with Noel, he caught me glancing at his secretary, her cleavage more than noticeable as she bent in front of us to bring us coffee. Not appropriate for the corporate setting. As she walked away Noel called me out, but just made it worse, crudely stating, "That's for me, not you." This approach to asserting his dominance was both unprofessional and demeaning. This incident made it clear Noel saw others, including me, as beneath him—a mindset that likely colored all his mentoring interactions.

This version of Noel's abuse of power didn't stop with inappropriate leering comments. During that same meeting Noel sought my input on whether he should fire Eric, a supervisor in our department. Noel's reasoning? He didn't like the way Eric "smelled," suggesting something must be wrong with him. At that point, I had only been with the company for three months, yet Noel the Controller was asking me to participate, to become his ally in what felt like a personal vendetta. The situation was a stark reminder that when mentors use their power for personal gain or to settle petty grievances, they can cause significant harm to those they are supposed to be guiding.

Another example of Noel-like behavior can be seen in mentors who guide their mentees down unethical paths for their own benefit. Recall how Ronnie pressured me to act against my moral compass to protect the company's financial interests and deceive a potential client. Noel the Controller is not just a bad mentor but a cautionary tale of what happens when mentorship goes wrong. This mentor stifles growth, instills fear, and manipulates situations to serve their own needs, leaving their mentee to navigate a treacherous professional landscape alone.

Managing the Malignant Mentors: Transcending the Toxicity

Dealing with malignant mentors requires vigilance and strategic handling, as these relationships, while initially supportive, can quickly turn toxic and destructive. You must be cautious of mentors like Harry the Hoarder, who prioritize their own advancement at the expense of their protégés, stunting others' growth to protect their positions. It's crucial to recognize when a mentor's self-interest outweighs their willingness to foster your development. Additionally, mentors like Lori the Loyalist may seem helpful but are ultimately more loyal to the company than to your personal growth, which can lead to betrayal and damage to your career. Finally, mentors like Noel the Controller embody the worst-case scenario, abusing their authority to dominate and manipulate, leaving mentees feeling trapped and unsupported.

What can we do? It's definitely easier said than done. Managing toxic would-be mentors requires stepping out of your comfort zone. To navigate these challenges, mentees must set clear boundaries, seek advice from multiple sources, and maintain control over their career paths to avoid becoming collateral damage in their mentors' power games.

Understanding the motivations of malignant mentors can shed light on their behavior and help determine whether they are inherently "bad" or simply acting out of misguided self-interest. These mentors are not always purely malicious; rather, their actions may stem from a complex mix of personal insecurities, career pressures, or a skewed sense of loyalty.

For instance, Harry the Hoarder might hoard opportunities because of a deep-seated fear of losing relevance or control. They may genuinely, but short-sightedly, believe their actions are necessary to secure their position or protect their team, even if this comes at the expense of the growth of their mentee and of their firm. Similarly, Lori the Loyalist might betray a mentee not out of malice but because their primary loyalty lies with the organization, and they believe that aligning with the company's interests is the best way to ensure everyone's survival, including their own.

Noel the Controller, on the other hand, might be driven by a desire for power and control, but this often reflects their own insecurities or past experiences where they felt powerless. They may justify their domineering behavior as a way to maintain order or achieve results, prioritizing those results over the people they work with and stifling the growth of those they mentor.

In many cases, these mentors are not entirely "bad" people; they may have moments of genuine support and good intentions. However, their actions become harmful when they allow their personal fears, ambitions, or misguided loyalty to overshadow their responsibilities as mentors. Understanding these motivations can help mentees navigate these relationships with more empathy and strategic thinking, recognizing when to engage, when to set boundaries, and when to seek guidance elsewhere.

Taking on and Taming the Mentoring Hydra

Dealing with all three categories of mentor monsters requires bravery, along with a careful balance of assertiveness, strategic thinking, and self-protection. Here are some recommendations for these situations and managing the relationships that otherwise might cause you to lose control over your career:

1. **Set Clear Boundaries**: From the outset, establish clear boundaries regarding your work, time, availability, and personal space. While you may be grateful to your mentor, you must also be firm in maintaining these boundaries to prevent your mentor from overstepping or becoming too controlling.
2. **Document Everything**: Save those emails! Keep detailed records of your interactions with the toxic mentor, including meetings, decisions made, and any questionable behavior. This documentation can be invaluable if you need to escalate the situation or protect yourself from potential backlash.
3. **Seek Multiple Perspectives**: Don't rely solely on your one mentor for advice or guidance. Build a network of mentors or colleagues inside your department and beyond (as presented in the INFUSE Framework in the next chapter) who can offer alternative perspectives and support. This helps you stay grounded and less dependent on one person's influence.
4. **Practice Self-Care**: Bad and imbalanced mentoring relationships can be emotionally draining. Prioritize your mental and physical well-being by engaging in activities that help you decompress and maintain a healthy work-life balance.

5. **Stay Professional**: Even in the face of toxic behavior, maintain your professionalism. Avoid reacting emotionally or engaging in confrontations that could escalate the situation. Keep communications respectful and focused on work-related matters.

6. **Leverage Allies**: Identify and connect with other colleagues or higher-ups who may share your concerns or have had similar experiences. Allies can provide support, offer advice, and help you navigate the toxic dynamics of monster mentors more effectively.

7. **Learn from the Experience**: While all kinds of relationships can be challenging, they can also be valuable learning experiences. Reflect on what you've observed, and use it to develop your own leadership and mentoring style. Sometimes we learn to do the opposite of what is done to us. This ensures we don't perpetuate monster mentoring behaviors in the future.

8. **Escalate When Necessary**: If your mentor's behavior crosses ethical or legal lines—such as harassment, discrimination, or unethical conduct—it's important to escalate the issue to HR, an ombudsman, or another appropriate authority. And continue to keep that paper or email trail. The reality is that, like your mentor, your friendly HR rep ultimately works for the company, not for you. Protecting yourself and others from harmful behavior is paramount.

9. **Develop Exit Strategies**: If the relationship becomes unbearable, have a plan in place to distance yourself from the monster mentor. This could involve seeking a transfer to another department, finding a new mentor, or even exploring opportunities outside the organization if necessary.

Chapter 8: The Mentoring Hydra

Most importantly, always keep your long-term career goals in focus. If a monster mentor is hindering your progress, take proactive steps to ensure your growth isn't stalled. Don't give up control. This might mean seeking new opportunities by changing jobs (as I did, moving from Eastland to TechFirm), even changing industries (as I did, moving from Corporate to Academia). The key is finding ways to bypass the mentor's negative influence. By employing these strategies, you can navigate the complexities of a monster mentoring relationship while minimizing its impact on your career and well-being.

Chapter 9: Your Mentoring Shopping Cart

In the introduction to this book, I asked you to consider this question: "If you could, what advice would you want to hear from your future self?" This is a complicated twist to the much-repeated question, "If you could, what advice would you give to your past self?"

Considering your future self is a complex exercise, which involves having an idea of what your future self even looks like. A mentor is a version of your future self. A mentor is someone who has already seen a lot of the things you are now dealing with. But here's the thing: mentors are important but really, they are a means to an end. You're still the one who's doing the work to control your career. Think of it like that classic saying by the legendary marketing scholar Ted Levitt: "You don't buy a drill just to have a drill, you buy a drill for the hole that it puts in the wall."

On one hand, who are we to argue? I still read this statement and hear it on podcasts all the time. You don't find a mentor simply to say you have one, you find a mentor to help you to have a positive outcome on your career and on your life. But Ted did not go far enough. You don't want to go around just putting holes in a wall. That's nonsense! You want an outcome, like building something new. Fixing something that's broken. Displaying something important to you, for others to see. To create something. You want an improvement, an outcome, not a hole in the wall. Once you've put that hole in the wall, you need a hammer, a screwdriver, and other tools to do the job right. It's the same with mentors. You don't collect mentors just to say you have them. And you need more than one mentor to help you build a career that you love.

INFUSE Framework

Mentoring is crucial for career growth, but finding and maintaining effective mentor relationships can be challenging. I'd like to introduce the INFUSE Framework, a new look to the fairly new approach of building a diverse mentor network. The idea of having multiple mentors represents quite a jump for you, going from possibly having none to ideally having several. This "developmental network" approach means having mentors from different backgrounds, each offering a wider range of perspectives and skills. If you open yourself up to the possibility of having multiple mentors, you can gain a more comprehensive understanding of the challenges that you will face, and you build a broader professional network. For instance, having mentors not just from different departments but also from different industries, and of different genders and ethnicities, can lead to higher career satisfaction and a stronger sense of belonging.

To follow the path of having multiple mentors, we have to rethink the word. A mentor can be anyone who contributes positively to your professional growth—whether they're an advisor, coach, trainer, sounding board, confidant, or even a friend. The key here is that these people help you gain and maintain control over your career. This is where the INFUSE Framework comes in, offering a structure for building a network of diverse and supportive relationships

Chapter 9: Your Mentoring Shopping Cart

Think of having a developmental network like creating a personalized "shopping cart" of mentors, each filling a specific role. Why am I calling it a shopping cart? Well, I am a marketing professor, so the retail analogy just feels right. But also, there is a selection process going on here. Just like you will select a particular product or service to suit your goals and needs, from among an array of possible purchases, you will also select the right mentors that suit your professional goals. To continue the shopping analogy, you don't just want to leave your mentors on the store shelf, you want them available and accessible to you. You are a consumer. And so are the mentors, who will also use their consumer decision-making tools to decide with whom they will work and with whom they will not. With this model in mind, we will examine six types of mentors or more specifically, mentoring relationships, you want to have in your shopping cart: industry peers, local contacts, company colleagues, supportive confidants, colleagues in similar roles, and exceptional role models.

The INFUSE Framework identifies six types of mentoring relationships to seek out:

- **Industry:** Someone from your field but not your firm.
- **Nearby:** Someone physically or virtually close to you.
- **Firm:** Someone from your own company.
- **Un- or Underrepresented:** Someone who is unique or exceptional in the way you are.
- **Similar:** Someone in a similar position to you, even if in a different industry.
- **Empathetic:** Someone who offers unwavering, empathetic support.

While these six categories conveniently spell out the word INFUSE, the relationships don't need to be pursued in any specific order. Also, one person might fulfill more than one role. For example, a mentor might be from your firm and also underrepresented in the same way as you. Similarly, you might receive empathetic support from both a spouse and a long-time friend. Knowing you don't have to fill your shopping cart in any specific order, and that one person can serve more than one role, relieves any pressure to find exactly one person who can do all these things, as well as from feeling like you need to find six different people to be your mentor. You might look at six people, or fewer, or more. It's the nature of these relationships that contributes to you having control of your career, that's what counts.

I: INDUSTRY

This might be one of the two most typical perceptions of a mentor: somebody in your INDUSTRY but not your firm. There are benefits to finding a mentor that understands how your industry works and has a broader set of experiences and perspectives beyond what you might find in your own work environment. Mentors in this category might be found at industry events, conferences, or from online communities the mentee participates or has participated in. Such mentors might also include past employers and colleagues.

While thinking about my situation and the difficulty I was facing at the end of my time at Chicagoland, my thoughts turned to the one paper I did publish. I mentioned this back in Chapter 7, titled "Consumer Grudgeholding: Toward a Conceptual Model and Research Agenda," in *The Journal of Consumer Satisfaction, Dissatisfaction and Complaining Behavior.* Grudgeholding. Within the business field of marketing and the narrower subfield of consumer behavior and the even narrower subcategory of consumer satisfaction, we are talking about a paper about an extremely niche topic appearing in a very niche journal. Beyond the topic of the paper, this story reveals another important mentoring tip: recognize the communities you belong to. The academic conferences I had been attending would host hundreds, even thousands of people. While my niche journal also hosted a conference, attendees numbered in the tens, not the hundreds. This was a small group of scholars laser-focused on consumer satisfaction and dissatisfaction and it was a community for me. And they had published my paper. So in the midst of my despair, I reached out to Keith, the editor of that journal, the one that had accepted my paper... and had accepted me.

When I let Keith know I was in the midst of losing my job at Chicagoland University, he told me countless outstanding faculty members had gone through, and are now going through, exactly what I'm experiencing. And that he can send me the names of some of those people as possible future collaborators. He reminded me there was nothing wrong with a slow start, as long as you start. And that he believed in me and there would always be a place for my next paper in his journal. I'm tearing up just thinking about it. He didn't have to do any of that. I never knew what it was like to get this kind of care and support from someone in my professional world. You might very well ask: What about Arnold? What about Phil? I took them for granted. I had blinders on and was so wrapped up in building, or saving, my career that I didn't realize how they were trying to help me do just that. But this response from Keith affected me in a way I had never experienced before. It reminded me of agapé, the Greek word for unconditional love. That is a word I did not know until graduate school and didn't really think about again until years later, upon reading the message from Keith. This kind of empathy, love, and support continues to inform my relationships. It also illustrates that there is plenty of opportunity for overlap in your mentoring relationships. Most importantly, Keith reminded me that I was not alone.

N: NEARBY

There are several clear advantages to having a mentor that is perceived to be nearby, readily accessible to you either through a quick walk down the hall or by picking up the phone for a call or text exchange. It is this kind of proximity that allows you and your mentor to discuss questions or have impromptu conversations and build a deeper relationship. Mentors in this category might also be part of the first group, that is, within the same industry. They might also be within the mentee's firm, the next category to be discussed. This once again illustrates the fact that overlaps in this model are possible. Arnold at TechFirm and Phil at Chicagoland both fit this description. Geoff and Tim did as well from my time at Northern Illinois University. The NEAR mentor might also be someone who is neither in your firm nor your industry. This mentor might be found in any one of the other five categories. I owe so much of my success and survival to a few dear friends of mine who are always just a text message away.

While having a mentor who is physically or virtually nearby can offer this kind of convenience and accessibility, there are also potential drawbacks. One might become overly dependent upon the mentor, leading to reduced independent problem-solving and decision-making. It's just too easy to run for help. Being so close can also lead to homogeneity, or a limited perspective. If your mentor is too similar to you in terms of background or experience, they might not effectively provide a different point of view, and may not challenge your thinking. Social pressure from outside your relationship can even have an impact. I believe that even after Jim left TechFirm three months after hiring me, I was still seen as "Jim's guy," which might have hindered me in developing my own identity even though Jim was nowhere near the building.

F: FIRM

A colleague from within your firm or department is another common source of mentorship. This type of relationship can be both formal, through company-sponsored programs, or informal, arising organically from interactions and shared experiences. Working with a mentor from your firm offers several benefits. First, you share the same work culture and a common understanding of the company's values, goals, and expectations. This can facilitate smoother communication and collaboration. You will also be likely to know shared experiences. Your colleagues are more likely to have had similar experiences and challenges, making them well-positioned to provide relevant advice and guidance. A mentor from within your firm will also be able to share their organizational knowledge. Mentors within the firm often have a more in-depth understanding of the company's structure, policies, and opportunities. And of course a mentor from within your firm is likely to be easily reached, fulfilling the NEARBY attribute of your mentoring relationships.

The possible drawbacks to working with a mentor in your own firm are similar to those listed for your NEARBY mentor. In addition, a mentor in your firm or department might be hesitant to provide critical feedback or advice that could negatively impact their own position. It's also important to recognize that if your mentor is a direct supervisor, there may be a power imbalance that could influence the mentoring relationship. Looking back, I wonder if this had an impact on my relationship with Phil. While Phil was not my supervisor, he was a tenured and well-established presence in my department. On the other hand, there were no such drawbacks on my relationships with Geoff and Tim, who were also tenured and well-established.

U: UNREPRESENTED

In this context, UNREPRESENTED (or UNDERREPRESENTED) refers to any trait that makes the mentee unique and possibly alone in their work environment. These characteristics, such as gender, ethnicity, religion, sexual orientation, physical appearance, personal presentation, or family status all can contribute positively to workplace diversity and offer distinct perspectives and experiences. However, they can also affect how one is perceived and treated in a professional setting. I would imagine that any of you who were the only woman, or only person of color, or felt compelled to fit in with the others while denying your true lived identity can understand the benefit somebody else like you might have provided. I vividly remember being the only person in a department of over 20 with childcare responsibilities, leading to a lack of support when meetings conflicted with caring for a sick child or getting to daycare on time. For example, when Lori the Loyalist betrayed my confidence at Chicagoland, it underscored the challenges of navigating such conflicts alone.

A mentor who represents in the same way as their mentee has often already navigated these difficult paths. Such mentors and allies can promote a sense of identity and community, counteracting feelings of isolation. Unfortunately, this type of mentor was nowhere to be found at Chicagoland, highlighting the need for representation to provide support and foster community in the workplace.

S: SIMILAR

Effective mentoring is built on trust and mutual understanding. This happens when mentors and mentees share SIMILAR experiences. A mentor with similar responsibilities or in a similar position to the mentee can offer the benefit of shared understanding and practical guidance. Whether in the same position, firm, industry, or even none of those, having a common set of challenges, and responsibilities can lead to a collaborative relationship. This level of commonality helps mentors offer practical guidance directly applicable to the mentee's current situation. When a mentor shares a similar role to the mentee, they offer a wealth of relatable experiences that will resonate with the mentee's own challenges and pressures. This common ground enables the mentor to offer advice and solutions that are not just theoretical but practically applicable to the mentee's specific situation. As opposed to Wes the Well-Intentioned, discussed in Chapter 8, a mentor in a similar role can offer support that is not out of context or past its expiration date.

A mentor with similar responsibilities offers guidance that really hits home. In a SIMILAR mentoring relationship, each participant might also be somebody else's mentee. Because they understand the ins and outs of the mentee's role—like the organizational dynamics and industry norms—they can tailor their advice to fit exactly what the mentee needs when they need it. This kind of insight is incredibly valuable, as it helps the mentee navigate their job with more confidence and clarity. On top of that, mentors in similar roles are key when it comes to building specific skills. They are concurrently seeking to master (or already have mastered) the same tasks—whether it's managing projects, leading a team, or making tough decisions—so they can share practical tips that match for the mentee's situation. Learning from someone who's been there or is still currently there means the mentee can quickly put these new skills to use in their own work.

In addition to skill development, these mentors offer crucial insights into potential career paths, whether or not they are working for the same firm. They can share ideas about what it takes to advance within a specific role or industry, drawing from their own experiences to highlight opportunities and warn against common pitfalls. This guidance helps the mentee navigate their career with greater clarity and purpose.

Finally, having a mentor with similar responsibilities can be a powerful confidence booster. Working with someone who is finding success or has effectively navigated similar challenges serves as a reminder that achievement and advancement are attainable, encouraging the mentee to take on new challenges with greater assurance. Additionally, such a mentor often brings a network of relevant contacts, expanding the mentee's support system and opening up new career opportunities.

There can be a downside to working with a mentor who is in a similar position as the mentee. What starts as a shared journey should be able to withstand one person leaving their job, but might buckle if both go for the same promotion only one person will get. This can lead to jealousy and resentment if not properly managed by the people involved. This can be made even more difficult when two former peers enter a relationship where one supervises the other.

In the best of circumstances, a mentor with similar responsibilities offers not just advice, but a roadmap for a shared journey that is directly applicable to the mentee's needs, making this relationship a cornerstone of professional development.

E: EMPATHY

Mentoring expert Kathy Kram defined a mentor as one serving as a sounding board and providing support. The INFUSE Framework recognizes the importance of EMPATHY in the support shared among the mentoring relationships.

Up until this point, I have shared only a few details about my relationship with Tim, from my time at NIU and beyond. Remember that I met Geoff first. He was the one who interviewed me on that fateful day in DeKalb and then pulled me out of my office to talk about my research. I met Tim shortly after I met Geoff, and worked closely with both of them. I continued to publish and make conference presentations with Tim until his recent retirement. One thing to keep in mind about Tim is that he taught at a rural school and hailed from an even more rural part of Illinois. This means Tim was about the last person I could possibly imagine to be a fan of legendary stoner comedians Cheech and Chong. Yet during the year I was at NIU, whenever I would run into Tim our encounters generally went something like this:

Me (to Tim): Hi Tim!

Tim (as Cheech): It's Dave! DAVE! Will you open up the bleepin' door!

Tim (also as Chong): Dave's not here, man.

Love ya, Tim! While Geoff tended to be rather direct in conversation (recall the very first words he said to me, that I had "taken a lot of bad advice"), Tim always had a compliment for me. It got to the point where I started to believe the nice things he would say to me! I would say both Geoff and Tim offered empathy that showed up as unconditional support to me… but maybe I had to work a little harder for Geoff. Love ya too, Geoff!

Empathy is the ability to understand and share another person's lived emotional experience, as if it were happening to you. Unlike unconditional support, which focuses on seeing someone in the best possible light, empathy involves truly feeling what the other person is going through. In this framework, empathy can show up as consistent encouragement, assistance, and advocacy. A mentor who offers empathetic support provides a safe space for emotional expression and reassurance, helping to boost your self-esteem and confidence when you need it most. This support fosters deeper, more honest conversations, and knowing you have an empathetic ally can help you build the strength and resilience needed to face your challenges more effectively.

As helpful as unconditional support can be, it can also lead to an overreliance, an addiction that can stunt your personal growth and independence. Too much support like this can also lead to your mentor not pushing you out of your comfort zone or providing the kinds of challenges you need to grow. Your relationship with a mentor demands a balance of support and challenge. While unconditional support can be invaluable, it's essential to ensure it doesn't hinder personal growth or create an unhealthy dynamic. Another drawback to a relationship like this can occur outside of the mentor-mentee relationship. If your mentor is in a position of authority, like a supervisor to you or others, the nature of your relationship might make those around you uncomfortable or even jealous. This can be damaging, if your coworkers think you aren't being held accountable, that you are your mentor's pet or puppet. Even with all the benefits unconditional support can provide, it is so important for the mentee to continue to build their own identity and professional development, as a strong colleague and not just a cipher.

Empathy and support are key benefits of this mentoring relationship. A mentor who has faced similar challenges offers a deep level of understanding and emotional support that can be especially comforting. This connection reduces the mentee's sense of isolation and bolsters their resilience.

GOING BEYOND YOUR "ROLODEX"

Don't worry if you don't know what a Rolodex is. Here's some business trivia for you: a Rolodex is a set of cards on a rotating device people used to use to store their contact information. Now we have apps for that, dozens of apps you can use in a much more efficient manner on your phone. Some (older) folks might still refer to their Rolodex even if they don't have one taking up space on their desk at work.

In the next two chapters we'll look at building your network so you can find the kinds of mentors to put in your shopping cart, whether you are part of a formal mentoring program or attempting to create the informal relationships that you need to develop. Mentorship is a cornerstone of professional development. By cultivating a diverse network or "shopping cart" of mentors from which to choose, you can accelerate your journey, enhance your skills, and gain invaluable insights while staying in control of your career. Regardless of your age or industry, mentors and mentorship programs, along with other relationships you build, offer you structure and a wide array of benefits that help you gain control over your career.

The INFUSE Framework provides a structured approach to building this network, emphasizing the importance of identifying and leveraging multiple mentor relationships. Mentoring helps employees by giving them the knowledge and guidance they need to plan for the future, build their skills, and handle workplace dynamics. This support lets mentees take charge of their careers and move closer to their professional goals. The INFUSE Framework of Mentoring Relationships makes it easier to identify the types of mentoring that work best for each person. It also shows that there's likely a strong network of potential mentors within your professional circle, which can make formal mentoring programs less necessary. In the end, the INFUSE Framework aims to shake up the traditional, more limited mentor-mentee relationship, helping people take control of their career paths and encouraging organizations to build a culture of mentorship and growth.

One more important point here. I want to reemphasize that you can and should have more than one mentor in your professional life. If you use the INFUSE Framework, you don't need all six mentors at once. You don't have to develop them in any particular order, even if they don't conveniently spell the word INFUSE on a piece of paper. In fact, the emphasis here is on the relationships that people offer you, not the number of people.

So if you have a Phil in your world, who is in the same FIRM and is NEARBY to you, please build that relationship, by taking and giving support. If you have Arnold, who checks several of those boxes (NEARBY, FIRM, SIMILAR) do likewise, but keep in mind that if your version of Arnold is your boss, as he was mine, they might have responsibilities that go beyond and might even run in conflict to your relationship. If you have a Keith, who is in your INDUSTRY but is less accessible and has traveled a very different path than yours, it is still up to you to keep that relationship alive. I did not do that and wish I had. And if you are fortunate enough to have someone like Geoff or Tim (NEARBY, FIRM, EMPATHY) pull you up off the floor and provide a much needed mentoring intervention, then you must take full advantage of their kindness, learn and grow and share what you have learned with others.

Chapter 10: Meriting a Mentoring Relationship

In order to keep greater control over your career, you can use the help of one or more mentoring relationships. This next chapter in our adventure together starts with a greater understanding about where you are now, what you expect from yourself, and about what others expect from you. And not only what others expect from you, but how you can exceed the expectations of others as well as your own.

Expectations. It's so hard to hit the mark when you can't see the target. Or when you don't even know what or where that target is. In that same way, it's hard to meet or exceed expectations when you aren't sure what those expectations are. That's how professional life started for me, and how I staggered along throughout the first half of my career. Since the start of what I've been calling the second half of my career, I've been fortunate enough to have several strong mentors to guide me. As for the first half, I blame my lack of strong, productive mentoring relationships mostly on my own professional clumsiness. I didn't ask for help. I didn't know who to ask, and I didn't know how to ask. I had no idea what was in my Superpower Portfolio or that I had any powers at all beyond just showing up. Don't get me wrong, showing up is quite important, but it's not enough. Your story thus far might be similar to my stumbling beginnings, even if you work in a different field. I truly hope what you've been reading so far leads you to a transition point in your career, much like Geoff and Tim's mentoring intervention caused a major transition in mine.

I got lucky, but you can't count on that. Luck can play a role in career success, but it's not a sustainable strategy. Yes, I'll celebrate my good luck in being rescued when my career was at its lowest. This was after I had to navigate through a complicated maze of missing, mismatched, and malignant mentors at Chicagoland, each offering advice that ranged from conflicting to selfish. It wasn't until I moved to NIU that I finally found the mentoring support I needed. Sometimes, you fall into the right opportunities, but you can't rely on chance to shape your career. While I haven't had another stroke of luck like that, I haven't needed it either. In the second half of my career, I've been fortunate enough to work with many more mentors. I've been proactive in seeking out mentors and building stronger, more intentional relationships aligned with my goals. Don't leave your career up to chance or the whims of others. Take control by actively developing and managing mentoring relationships. Luck is fleeting and can't be counted on; becoming a vector through your own self-direction is sustainable. This all comes from stepping out of your comfort zone, to where you are still safe and ready to grow.

And how can you do this? How can you bring about your own transition? How can you make sure your trajectory is pointing up? By gaining the courage to understand your comfort zone, where you are right now, and then moving outside of and expanding your comfort zone. And if your comfort zone doesn't feel all that comfortable right now? We're going to talk about that too.

Stretched Beyond Comfort Yet Still Safe

A few chapters back, I told you about my work with the Walter & Connie Payton Foundation. What I didn't tell you was how this client relationship came to be, and how it involved stepping way out of my comfort zone, far beyond the border but still in a place where I was safe.

When I was working at Chicagoland, I lived 35 miles away and frequently took the train to work. This meant getting up extra early, fighting for a parking space at the station, and then sitting in a crowded train car. The train would bring me to Union Station in Chicago, about a mile walk from our building. This situation was not conducive for getting any work done, even though I usually tried to anyway. To make matters even worse, sometimes I'd be next to someone having a loud conversation on their phone, making it even harder to relax, read, write, or whatever futile attempt at productivity I made. This was the case one fall day, when the lady sitting next to me was on the phone but might as well have been shouting to her friend across the train car.

Jackie turned out to be a very kind person and wonderful to work with. I do mention this because, Jackie, I wasn't trying to listen in on your private conversation. I really had no choice. When Jackie was on her call, I kept hearing her referring to a couple of people named Walter and Connie. If you are not from Chicago, that might not mean a lot to you. But to me, as a Chicago Bears fan, I knew she was referring to the Bear's legend Walter Payton and his wife Connie. And despite my love for my beloved Bears, it would have been very easy to shake my head and simply walk off the train after it pulled into the station, and begin my long walk to work. That would have been well within my comfort zone, which at that time too often meant not networking and not introducing myself to people who might be good for me to meet.

But I stepped out of my comfort zone. I gently walked up alongside Jackie. "Excuse me, ma'am... I'm a marketing professor at Chicagoland and I'm sorry, but I overheard some of your conversation. Are you working with the Payton Foundation?" I have a feeling she might have felt pushed out of her comfort zone too, being drawn into a conversation with a strange guy as soon as she stepped off the train, probably on her way to an important meeting. That's why I introduced myself as a marketing professor. That was my way of letting her know right away that I might be of some use to her. It's amazing how a simple, respectful introduction—like mentioning your profession, or areas of expertise, or simply something you have in common, can break the ice with a perfect stranger and set a positive tone for conversation.

Comfort Zone, Transition Zones, and the Two Crescent Model

Your Comfort Zone

In a professional context, the comfort zone is the condition where you feel capable, at ease, and in control of your work and your surroundings. Within this space, tasks and challenges are familiar, minimizing stress and risk but often limiting growth and innovation. Your comfort zone lies within the boundaries you set for yourself.

There are some good reasons to protect your boundaries and stay in your comfort zone. Working where you feel comfortable can offer you stability and reduce the stress you might feel. You can become better at what you are doing, gaining depth of knowledge and expertise. All this can make you more effective and productive. You might feel like you are in control over a limited domain. While staying in the comfort zone can provide stability, stepping outside of it is often necessary for growth. I would not be surprised if you've read or heard that before, and not only in an earlier chapter of this book. It seems like everybody is telling you, and surely everybody knows, that outside of your comfort zone you'll discover glorious career advancement, skill development, and amazing new opportunities.

Let's take a different approach to understanding your comfort zone. For illustration, let me share my two-crescent comfort zone model. Start with a circle, as most depictions of the comfort zone tend to do. That circle represents your comfort zone, home to the way you might be living your life right now, both professionally and personally. Inside this zone are the activities and projects that are comfortable to you, that you do all the time.

Other depictions of your comfort zone promise you that way outside of your comfort zone is where the magic happens. We're not looking for magic, we're looking for real growth. To that end, we draw a second circle, overlapping the first. We won't worry about the relative sizes of the circles or by how much they overlap, not yet anyway. The answers to those questions vary by person and situation. We might be more willing to step out of our own comfort zones in some situations than in others. Now you can see with our two overlapping circles, our Venn diagram has three areas. We started with the first circle, your comfort zone. Now let's examine the two new areas, both crescent-shaped. We can draw these circles vertically, as I did below, or going from right to left or left to right. There's no wrong answer.

The key is that we see two new crescent-shaped zones, one outside of your comfort zone and another still inside of that original circle.

Safe Zone

COMFORT ZONE

Deception Zone

Your Safe Zone

First let's look at your safe zone. No matter how you drew up your two circles, there is likely a large overlap between your safe zone circle and your original comfort zone. That just makes sense, that it's safe to do what you are comfortable doing, what you've been doing. Here's one crucial point: you can still be safe outside of your comfort zone. This may not be the case 100% of the time, but it is true surprisingly often. Think about it. What are some things you have done and achieved that, looking back, you realize you may have actually stepped outside of your comfort zone? And what are some things you have been hesitating to do that, if you think about it, are probably pretty safe after all? You've seen other people take chances... high or even medium probability of success-type chances... and you can too. You can be safe outside of your comfort zone. These memes and illustrations are true. When you take a chance, a little beyond your headlights but still safe, what was once seen as risky is now comfortable. Think about the worst that can happen... and how the reward might outweigh the risk!

Your Deception Zone

Now take another look at our Venn diagram. There is another crescent, on the opposite side of the safe zone but still within the comfort zone. That means your activities in this zone feel comfortable but can actually cause trouble. That's why I label this crescent the deception zone. Your comfort zone covers what you do every day. It's what you're good at. It's what makes you comfortable. Like a merry-go-round, you're moving around but not moving forward. Have you become too comfortable with activities, behaviors, routines that aren't safe or aren't good for you? Or they keep you comfortable but stunt your growth, blind you to opportunities? Some of your work might still fall within your comfort zone, but they might not necessarily be good for you.

Do you have any behaviors or habits that fall into the Deception Zone? Sometimes we do things just because we always have. That doesn't necessarily mean they're dangerous, but you might be using resources in a way that slows you down, leads to stagnation... and that can be dangerous. You might think you're making progress when you're not. Complacency and false confidence can lead you to believe you're growing when, in reality, you're standing still or going backwards as those around you move forward. It is important to recognize when you're in this zone. Stay aware, and don't confuse busy work with real development.

Transition Zones: Moving Beyond Comfort

There is another important part of our two-crescent comfort zone model. It's one thing to say "go outside of your comfort zone." If it were that easy, we wouldn't need all these memes and articles about going outside of your comfort zone. There are lines between all three of these areas, dividing the comfort and the safe zones, and dividing the comfort and deception zones. Let's call these borders our transition zones. Take a look at our illustrations. You might not have even been thinking about the lines around the circles you drew. So now is the time that we focus on those divisions.

Transition zones might just look like the lines that create your circles, but in our two-crescent comfort model, these lines represent the areas between comfort and new growth and between comfort and stagnation. They may be thick or thin, deep or shallow, complex or simple. And they might be what keeps you from moving forward. Transition zones are more than just lines you cross. They involve mental and emotional shifts, sometimes more challenging than expected. Each transition is unique. When you are moving out of your comfort zone, it's one thing to look at a diagram that says you are still safe, but quite another to actually take that step over the line, outside of your comfort zone. There are several reasons why we might stay in our comfort zones, unwilling or unable to cross that transition line even though it is still safe.

- **Risk aversion**. Some of us embrace risk and love to take changes, while others prefer to play it safe. It's important to realize this might apply to you more in some situations than others. While you might see that some people are always walking on the razor's edge, I'm sure in certain situations you might be more willing to take a risk than in others.

- **Fear of the unknown.** You know what's in your comfort zone. You don't know what's in your safe zone, and you won't know until you see for yourself.
- **Imposter Syndrome.** You might not feel you're qualified to leave your comfort zone... in fact, you might feel like you don't belong in your safe zone either. This is where our Superpower Portfolio and You Own Your Origin story work from earlier comes into play. The most daunting part about stepping over the transition zone line into the safe zone might be in your head.

In contrast, the reason we might stay in our deception zone is we might not even realize we're there. The deception zone still feels safe and we can't or won't see the danger that slipping backward can lead to. Just as stepping out of our comfort zone into our safe zone makes both of them bigger and more welcoming, staying in our deception zone can make our comfort zone smaller and more limited, and the safe zone that much further away. Overcoming the constraints of staying in the deception zone, where we feel safe but are unaware of the hidden risks or stagnation, requires a combination of self-awareness, external feedback, and proactive strategies. Here are some ways to break free from this zone:

- **Reflection.** Regularly assess where you are in your career or life. Journaling, mindfulness practices, structured self-assessments, and even talking with a trusted friend or mentor can help identify areas where you may be stagnating without realizing it.
- **Identify Signs of Stagnation.** Look for subtle signs such as feeling too comfortable or even bored. Are you not being challenged, or are you avoiding new opportunities out of fear? Recognize these patterns of complacency and

boredom as potential indicators that you're in the deception zone.

- **Peer Accountability.** Engage in peer feedback from colleagues or peers who understand, empathize with, and can relate to your goals. They can help challenge your perceptions and encourage you to stretch beyond what you consider safe.
- **Small Steps.** Start by setting goals that feel slightly uncomfortable but not overwhelming. These can expand both your comfort and safe zones without making the leap feel too risky.
- **Seek Opportunities.** Make a commitment to seek projects, tasks, or learning opportunities that push your current abilities, even if they cause some discomfort or fear of failure.
- **Reframe.** Instead of seeing failure as a setback, reframe it as part of growth. Recognizing even your mistakes can provide learning experiences that help you advance from your deception zone to your comfort zone, and from your comfort zone to your safe zone.
- **Growth mindset.** Continuously explore new skills, ideas, and perspectives. By fostering curiosity and a love for learning, you'll be more inclined to leave the deception and comfort zones behind as you seek growth opportunities.

By now, you know your relationships with mentors can be the key to crossing through your transition zones. Mentoring happens in the transition zones. Think of it like this: if you are in a comfort zone or a deception zone, you probably aren't looking for any help. A trusted mentor or coach can help you see blind spots and areas where you might be fooling yourself into thinking you're progressing when you're not. They can provide a reality check and help identify challenges and opportunities you may be ignoring. You should continue to strive to build a network of mentors who push you beyond your current boundaries. They can introduce new ideas and opportunities that force you to step out of deception and comfort and into intentional action.

Gaps Analysis

As we expand our comfort zone by crossing into our ever-growing safe zone, we have to assess where we need help and where we may still be falling short. This is where a gaps analysis comes in. By identifying the areas where we need support or improvement, we can ensure our growth is purposeful and aligned with our goals. Stepping out of the comfort zone is a powerful first step, but to truly advance and grow, we must also evaluate where we may need help. A gaps analysis helps us to pinpoint those areas, allowing us to close the distance between where we are and where we want to be. We know we have superpowers and we also know we have flaws. Self-awareness is key. You know your strengths, but you also need to understand your weaknesses.

First, a definition. A gaps analysis is simply looking at the gaps, the distance, between where you want to be and where you are. What you want to do, and what you're doing. What you need and what you're getting. Let's explore how to recognize these gaps so you can strategically build mentor relationships that support your growth. In our context, a gaps analysis is simplified to examining three key points in your professional life and the gaps between them. Two gaps between three different points:

1) What is expected of you?

2) What are you trying to do?

3) What are you accomplishing?

And so just like if you draw each of those points in a line on a piece of paper, you'll see three points and two gaps.

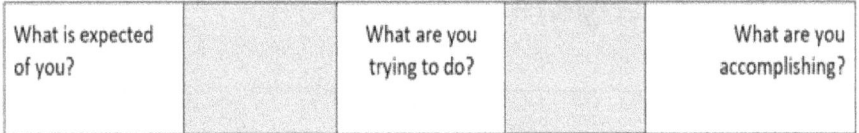

What is expected of you?		What are you trying to do?		What are you accomplishing?

a) The gap between what is expected of you and what you are trying to do.

b) The gap between what you are trying to do and what you are accomplishing.

Let's start with that possible first gap, the gap between what your boss or client expects from you, and what you think they expect from you. Sometimes, what's expected of you by your employer, peers, or mentors doesn't align with what you're currently focused on. This gap can lead to wasted effort or unmet expectations. Just as a quick aside, this might have been THE biggest gap I experienced at TechFirm. Jim, the person who hired me, the person who I hoped would mentor me and teach me, was fired just three months after I started. I was young, quite naïve, so I didn't know what I was supposed to do.

After Jim left and I failed to stay in touch, I just assumed somebody else would know what I was supposed to do next. They would know, and they would tell me. But I realized nobody else really knew what I was hired for. As strange as it sounds, this is a big reason why we're here together right now, to help you understand and manage expectations. Because if there is a gap between what IS expected of you and what you THINK is expected, what you spend your time and energy doing, you might find yourself running in the wrong direction, doing things that get you nowhere, that aren't rewarded, that aren't expected or desired from you.

How do you find out what your boss, your customer, your clients, or your director need? How do you find out what they expect from you? It might be in your job description. If you have one. But the gap between your job descriptions and what you are expected to do will change over time, as the corporate and environmental worlds change, and as you grow into your job. Is it possible you want to do things that maybe aren't on that description, that aren't expected of you? And if you're not working currently, you can still take this approach toward your job search or even your own personal goals. Do you understand what you expect of yourself? This is a huge question we must ask of ourselves. This is gap one in our gaps analysis. If you find that there's a big gap between what you think you're expected to do and what the other person wants, there might be a whole new conversation that has to come from it. And if there's a lot that you want to do that isn't expected of you, that's another conversation for you to have before you stagnate.

Gap two is the gap between what you are trying to do and what you are actually accomplishing. We're moving past expectations now, to actually try to figure out how you're going to do your job even better. This is the gap between what you are doing and the outcomes you experience. Are your actions leading to the desired results and outcomes? Are you delivering? Is your work taking you where you're supposed to go? Are the outcomes matching your actions, that might be the simplest way to look at it. Again, we're focusing on gaps between what you are trying to do and how those plans turn out. If this gap exists, if you find things don't always go as you plan, you are not alone. There are some good reasons for this. It might be that you're still learning how things work in your company or department. Sometimes it might be because there are other people involved that maybe didn't do things the way you expected them to.

This is important, because that could mean there's another gap, a gap in communications between you and whoever is next in line on the project you're working on. It could be you didn't explain it well enough. It could be the people you're working with chose to take things in a different direction. Things change once they leave your hands. And so a good habit to get into is to continue frequent, solid, thorough, meaningful, and open-minded communication with the people you're working with. When you think you've set something in motion, it's important to see it actually gets carried out that way. Follow through. Because really, the way things turn out, that's what people see. That's what the customer sees. That's what your boss sees. That's what your client sees. That's what your colleagues see.

Think about examples in your own experience of when things turned out the way you planned… and when they didn't. What might be some factors involved? Were different people or departments involved, different numbers of people? Did you plan differently in these cases? Other internal or external factors in play? Think about your own experiences, where maybe you meant to do something one way but it turned out a different way, for better or for worse. And again, note what's happening after a request, a ticket, or project leaves your hands. Finally, are your accomplishments being recognized? If not, this could represent a gap in visibility. A mentor can guide you in understanding how to advocate for yourself, increase your visibility within your organization, and ensure your contributions are valued and rewarded.

Chapter 10: Meriting a Mentor Relationship

A gaps analysis is an effective tool to diagnose areas where development is needed within your current role or future goals. It's a simple thought process that helps identify areas where you can strengthen your skills, refine your actions, and ensure you're on track to meet both personal and professional objectives. By identifying these gaps, you can also assess whether you're being compensated fairly for your efforts and whether your current role aligns with your growth aspirations. By recognizing these gaps, you can take proactive steps to ensure your efforts are aligned with expectations, that you're working toward meaningful achievements, and your contributions are recognized and rewarded.

You don't have to do all this alone. This is where you have to seek and find help from others. This is what I described in the last chapter when I shared the INFUSE Framework of mentoring. To make the most of INFUSE, you have to examine the gaps you discovered. What kind of help do you need? Let's review your options as spelled out in the Framework. Do you need to talk to someone in your same **industry** but with enough distance from your own department or company to offer that outsider perspective? Do you need somebody **nearby** you can talk to right away? Maybe even someone within our own **firm** that can help you navigate your situation. Perhaps you are feeling isolated and need to reach out to somebody who is **underrepresented** in the same way you are. Somebody who has walked a **similar** path as you are facing. Or just someone with **empathy**, to lend an ear. And remember, this can mean one person or several. And now you have to act. You have to reach out. Here's how.

Your Presence

To understand how to build on and even create new mentoring relationships, we need to talk about your presence. How do you establish your presence in front of or alongside the people you're working for and working with? It's not simply by asking, by showing up at somebody's desk; you've got to do more than that. As a quick aside, I want to share some of the worst advice I got early in my career from one of my mentoring monsters. And this advice might sound familiar to you, especially when you're in a new situation. That advice was "Keep your head down." And what does that mean?

It means this: stay out of the way, don't get involved, stay out of danger, stay out of conflicts that might have a longer history than you do at a particular organization. Be seen and not heard, and maybe even not seen. Play it safe. Play it safe, huh? Well, I took that advice. And I regret staying out of the way. Keeping your head down means not letting people know what you're doing and what you're good at. It means hiding what you are contributing, and how you are willing to take your talents, your strengths, which we've been talking about, and applying them to the situation in front of you. It means you are not letting people know you are there and you have something important to offer. Bad idea!

Instead, I encourage you to establish your presence. Say yes to everything. Now, hang on a second... "everything"? EVERYTHING, everything? This might sound like a big change and a big risk. A huge step out of your comfort zone. It's a good thing we went over all of this earlier in this very chapter. If you're like me, managing your time is already enough of a challenge. And beyond the day-to-day, you might think if you say yes to everything, you'll be swamped, you'll be overwhelmed, you won't have time to do other things that might be more important than all the things you said yes to. Fair enough.

So let's modify that a little bit. Let's just say you should walk around with a "say yes" attitude. Go into each day, each meeting, each encounter, with the mindset of saying yes, not saying no. If somebody comes up to you with a project, you don't have to blurt out, "Yes, I'll do it! Now, what is the project again?" The say yes attitude means you carry with you a mindset of *How can I do this? How can we be a team, how can we collaborate, how can I bring this into my world and share my talents and my strengths with somebody who clearly wants me to do just that, who needs me to share my strengths, to help them with my superpowers?*

You know if you're being asked to do something, it's probably because the person who is asking thinks you can do it and do a good job on it. Or maybe they think, well, this will be a stretch for you. And that's not a bad thing. Accept that compliment. It's important for you to realize that whether someone is delegating a task to you or asking for your help with a project, that person is demonstrating trust in you. They believe in you. And they are willing to risk some of their own reputation on your ability to succeed. Take that as praise because it is.

Not long ago, we talked about your comfort zone. And one reason I say "say yes to everything" is because this might include some things that are in your comfort zone and some things that maybe are not in your comfort zone, making you stretch. For right now, your next step is to think about the projects and opportunities in front of you. Whether you've written them down or not at this point, keep or start writing them down, add them to your list of strengths, your list of goals. And think about how saying yes, going with a positive, optimistic, can-do ambitious, motivated, growth mindset... coming from **inside** of you... can make a difference in your interactions with other people and your achievements. You can be recognized as someone the people around you can count on.

When you say yes to something you have got to follow through... and you can do it. Adopt that mindset. You still have to manage your life and manage your work and manage your time. But this step here is to look at that list of goals, look at the projects you've built, look at the expectations we've developed over the past few pages. And think about this: what can you say yes to internally? What have you been stalling on, hesitating on, and maybe lacking confidence in? Turn that attitude around, say yes to everything. Including yourself. What opportunities are in front of you, waiting for you to say "Yes"? Make your plan to contribute, whether verbally or nonverbally.

Now, establishing your presence... that might take you out of your comfort zone. Remember, though, your real rewards are in your safe zone. And one of those rewards may very well be this opportunity to find a mentor. So now I want to help you take a GIANT step... that is, if you haven't already taken that step on your own. Are you saying "yes" to building your mentoring relationships?

Take The Giant Step

It's time to take action. Start by creating a list of mentors you can reach out to. This list should reflect the diversity of your INFUSE Framework. Remember, you don't have to match all six kinds of relationships right away, and you don't have to do it in any particular order. Choose someone to contact. This could be through a call, an email, a coffee chat, or even a Zoom meeting. This person might become your mentor—they just don't know it yet. You can start with someone you aspire to, someone you don't know well but hope to work with or be like some day. If you're feeling hesitant, start with people you already know and trust. Strengthen those relationships first. Both approaches are valid. When reaching out, don't feel the need to label the relationship right away. You're not going to lead with, "Hey, will you be my mentor?" That might come across as too formal or forced. Mentorship grows organically— it's something both people discover, develop, and desire over time.

Remember, there's a strong element of marketing in mentoring. You want to position yourself as someone worth investing time and resources in. The mentor should feel your growth and success are worth their efforts, just as you should feel that they bring something valuable to your journey.

Mentors, too, have motivations:

- They may value your insights as a sounding board or potential future hire.
- They might enjoy the personal satisfaction of helping others like you.
- Or, they may seek to create a legacy, experiencing what psychologists call generativity—the desire to pass on knowledge and shape the next generation.

If this sounds idealistic, trust that this dynamic does happen— and it could happen to you too.

When you meet with your potential mentor, make sure your strengths and what you have to offer are evident in the conversation. This is about a mutual exchange.

Starting the Conversation

Your first and early conversations with potential mentors are not contract negotiations. This is not about walking into someone's office with a list of demands. It's about building a natural, authentic relationship where both of you feel comfortable, share openly, and help each other grow.

Here's how you can initiate that connection:

Step 1: Don't ask directly.

You don't need to say, "Will you be my mentor?" Instead, start with small steps: get to know each other, share ideas, ask questions.

Step 2: Email is a good place to start.

Although phone calls are more personal, people are harder to reach by phone these days. Email works, though both calls and messages may be screened by gatekeepers. So, your challenge is to craft an effective message.

How to Craft Your First Email:

10. **Request a brief meeting.** Ask if they can spare 30 minutes for a conversation. Keep the message and the proposed meeting short, so everything feels manageable. If the meeting runs longer than planned, that's a good sign.
11. **Acknowledge their expertise.** Be clear about what you're seeking and why. Is it advice on navigating your career? Understanding departmental politics? Exploring a new industry? Make your request specific and thoughtful.
12. **Respect their time.** Reassure them you're prepared and you value their time. Mentors are often busy, and it's important to show you're serious about making the most of the opportunity.

Chapter 10: Meriting a Mentor Relationship

After Sending the Message

Once you've sent the email or left your message, be patient. The ball is in their court, and they might not reply right away—or at all. If you don't hear back, follow up after one or two weeks, but don't persist too much. If they decline to talk to you, that's okay. It's happened to me, too. Try again with someone else. Or, politely ask the same person once more at a later time. No guilt tripping, no blaming. Every interaction must come from a place of respect.

When the mentor you seek does say "yes," congratulations! You've started to overlap your lives, and now it's time to set up that first meeting—whether in person, over coffee, or online. Be flexible with their schedule and come prepared.

Building the Relationship

In your first few meetings, focus on building rapport. Don't rush into labeling the relationship as a mentorship. Just as you are getting to know them, they are getting to know you. Trust and rapport take time to develop. In fact, you might realize the person you have been pursuing is not an ideal mentor for you, or might be, but at a later time. Don't be discouraged. This is good to know early on. If this relationship is worth keeping for any reason, then find reasons to stay in contact. Continue reaching out and nurturing other potential relationships. Even if someone doesn't become your mentor, sending them interesting articles or notes every few months can help keep the relationship alive.

That holds especially true if you decide you want to build a relationship with this new mentor. Once the relationship is established, schedule regular feedback sessions. These provide an opportunity to reflect on your progress, address challenges, and adjust your goals as needed.

Take Another Giant Step... and then Another

I hope these chapters have been both inspirational and empowering, giving you greater control over your career. Take a moment to reflect on how far you've come. You've built your Superpower Portfolio, identified areas for growth, and taken meaningful steps to shape your career with intention. This journey wasn't just about reading, but about embracing the power of mentorship and self-awareness. You've gained valuable insights into building relationships and understanding your unique abilities—qualities that make you not only a strong mentee with a great deal to offer others, but also a future mentor. This is no small achievement, and your dedication deserves recognition. As I often say in my workshops: you are a vector, with both direction and magnitude.

And a vector doesn't stay still. Now is the time to put the insights and lessons into practice. It's one thing to understand the value of mentorship, but it's another to take the giant step of seeking it out. Reaching out to a potential mentor, initiating that first conversation, or even scheduling a simple coffee chat can feel intimidating, but remember: you've already done the hard work of preparing yourself. By building your Superpower Portfolio and reflecting on your unique origin story, you've equipped yourself with the self-awareness and confidence to form authentic connections. It's normal to hesitate stepping out of your comfort zone but that shouldn't hold you back. Your readiness isn't about being perfect; it's about being prepared and open to growth. Now is the time to step forward, take action, and pursue the mentoring relationships that will support your continued success.

As you continue your journey, an exciting new chapter awaits—one where you step into the role of mentor. Mentorship is a two-way street, a cycle of giving and receiving. As you seek guidance, you'll also find opportunities to share your own experiences with others. This next stage isn't just about helping others grow, it's about deepening your own learning. Becoming a mentor reinforces the lessons you've gained as a mentee and strengthens your skills. As you'll see in the next chapter, mentoring is a powerful way to build your legacy and give back. Get ready to see how guiding others can be as transformative for you as it is for them.

So take action—reach out to someone in your universe who can help you grow. Remember, mentorship is a journey, and starting that conversation is key. This isn't the end of your path, but the beginning of a new phase. The next chapter will guide you into the world of mentorship, where you'll continue to grow by inspiring others while also helping you take that important next step.

Chapter 11: Growing Into a Mentor

You've come a long way on this journey with me, and I'm proud to play some role in your ability to find the kind of mentoring relationships that will move your arrow up and forward. I like to see growth, yours and mine, as a vector. Vector is a physics term depicted as an arrow, which conveys direction and magnitude. Throughout this book, my intention has been to help you understand and develop your sense of your magnitude. And as a mentee, your journey will be shaped by the directions of guidance provided by your mentors, pointing you toward new opportunities and greater confidence. Now, as you reflect on the path you've taken and look ahead to the path that is in front of you, it's clear that your own vector has gained strength. While your direction is still being determined and may change as you continue to grow, the magnitude of what you've learned is undeniable. With that power comes the responsibility to give back—to become the mentor who can help guide others. Just as you will be helped toward success, you will soon have the chance to shape the vectors of those who follow in your footsteps.

Your Relationships Are Evolving

According to mentoring expert Kathy Kram (1985), mentoring relationships typically progress through four distinct stages: initiation, cultivation, separation, and redefinition. In the **initiation phase**, which generally lasts the first 9 to 12 months, the foundation of the relationship is built, as both the mentor and mentee begin to establish trust and rapport. This is followed by the **cultivation phase**, which can extend from one to five years. During this time, the relationship deepens as the mentor provides guidance, support, and opportunities for growth. Eventually, the relationship reaches a point of **separation**, when it is time to begin disengaging. This stage can be marked by a sense of loss, but it also reflects the mentee's growing independence. Finally, the relationship may enter the stage of **redefinition**, where the dynamic shifts, and the mentee starts to relate to their mentor as more of a peer than as their elder, boss, or superior.

Keep in mind that your situation may be different. Your relationships might start and evolve faster, slower, smoother, rougher, than others, involving more than one mentoring relationship at a time and even with the occasional mentoring monster lurking. As individuals grow, and the relationship matures, adjusting your interactions and support will occur. As you grow in your career and start to see what your path looks like with more clarity, your relationship with your mentors will inevitably evolve. What began as a traditional mentor-mentee dynamic, where your mentoring relationships combined to provide the kinds of guidance, teaching, support, and expertise, will transform into a more peer-like relationship. As you gain experience and confidence, the once-clear distinction between mentor and mentee blurs. You'll find yourself contributing more to the relationship, perhaps offering insights and feedback that reflect your own growing expertise. This shift can be both exciting and challenging as it requires a recalibration of how you engage with your mentor. Also keep in mind that those who have been your mentors might start dedicating more time to new mentees who are earlier in their journeys.

When this evolution happens, it's important to ask yourself if it's time to redefine or even reduce the scope of the mentoring relationship. Some mentors may naturally step back as you take on more responsibility, while others may remain active partners in your development, offering guidance but on a more equal footing. It's critical to recognize when the nature of the relationship has shifted and to openly discuss those changes. What worked when you were just starting may no longer be necessary or even relevant as your own goals and capabilities expand.

Managing these modified relationships requires clear communication and mutual respect. Whether it's a formal meeting as part of a formal program, or just a kind of unspoken realization, recognizing this shift—from mentee to near-peer—demonstrates maturity and awareness of your own growth. You may need to recalibrate expectations, define new boundaries, and determine the kind of support you still need. At the same time, you should be prepared to offer value back to your mentor, whether through your unique perspectives, industry insights, or collaborative projects. In doing so, you not only honor the relationship but also lay the groundwork for a more balanced, reciprocal partnership.

The Mentoring Hydra - Revisited, Resisted

Before we finish, I want to remind you of the various archetypes of mentors to avoid: Missing Mentors, Mismatched Mentors, and Malignant Mentors. Each represents a type of relationship that can hinder your growth and derail your career rather than support it. By recognizing these behaviors in those who might be your mentors, and in yourself, you can better navigate your mentoring relationships and ensure they contribute positively to your career.

Missing Mentors

By now, you've seen how frustrating it can be to deal with a 'Missing Mentor'—someone who seems promising at first but then disappears, leaving your calls and emails unanswered. As you grow into a mentor yourself, remember how crucial it is not to become the very type of mentor you found frustrating. Stay engaged, be communicative, and never underestimate the impact of following through. Being present and proactive isn't just a courtesy—it's the foundation of a meaningful mentoring relationship.

To avoid becoming a Missing Mentor, start by setting clear expectations with your mentee from the beginning. Even better, encourage them to take the lead on this assignment. Be realistic about your availability and boundaries, and create a mutual understanding of how often and in what format you'll stay in touch. Regular check-ins, even brief ones, can make all the difference in maintaining the relationship.

Also, consider the mentee's perspective, because whether they are new to your industry or experiencing uncertainty, they will rely on you for guidance. The inconsistency of a mentor can lead to self-doubt or frustration, leaving the mentee questioning their worth or progress. Avoid this by being reliable and present, even during your busiest times if for only a few minutes. If you find yourself unable to engage as often as you'd like, be transparent about it and suggest alternative sources of support or guidance.

Finally, remember that your mentorship is not just about being available when things are going well; it's about showing up when your mentee is facing challenges. Offer reassurance during difficult times and follow up on their progress after setbacks.

Mismatched Mentors

A missing mentor is one thing, but a mismatched mentor requires a different approach. These individuals aren't necessarily avoiding you, but their advice or methods may not suit your needs. As you evolve into a mentor, remember how crucial it is not to become a poor match for your mentee. Be mindful of your mentee's goals, offer advice that empowers their growth, and ensure your relationship is rooted in mutual respect and trust, rather than simply transactional exchanges. The best mentoring comes from listening, understanding, and adapting to the needs of your mentee.

To avoid becoming a mismatched mentor yourself, take the time to truly understand where your mentee is coming from. Don't assume what worked for you will automatically work for them. Ask thoughtful questions to uncover their unique challenges and aspirations. Your role as a mentor is to guide them along their path, not necessarily to force them down the same dusty road you once traveled. Offer advice tailored to their situation, and recognize when your perspective may not align with their specific needs. It's also important to check in regularly about the relationship itself. Ask your mentee if they feel the guidance you're providing is helping them meet their goals. Be open to feedback and adjust your approach if necessary. A good mentor knows the relationship is a two-way street. Even as you share your expertise, you should also be open to learning from your mentee's experiences.

Malignant Mentors

The most dangerous mentors are what I call the malignant mentors. Relationships with these would-be guides can become toxic, leading to unexpected, detrimental outcomes for your career. Dealing with these relationships requires stepping outside of your comfort zone. Setting boundaries, seeking guidance from other mentors, and maintaining control over your career path are essential strategies for protecting yourself from becoming collateral damage. As you prepare to step into the role of mentor, remember how critical it is not to become a malignant mentor yourself. Stay focused on the well-being and growth of your mentee, rather than your own advancement. Avoid letting external pressures or insecurities cloud your judgment. Remember why you are becoming a mentor in the first place. By prioritizing genuine, supportive relationships and ensuring your mentees feel valued and empowered, you can become the kind of mentor who inspires and uplifts, rather than one who limits and stifles.

To avoid becoming a malignant mentor, self-awareness is key. Regularly reflect on your motivations and actions in the mentor-mentee relationship. Are you giving advice that serves the best interest of your mentee, or are you subtly prioritizing your own career goals or personal gain? It's natural to feel pressure from your own job or external challenges, but it's important to separate those pressures from your mentoring responsibilities. Ensure your guidance remains centered on the mentee's growth and success. Additionally, practice transparency. Be open with your mentee about any conflicts of interest, especially in formal work settings where your loyalty may be split between the organization and the individual. Clarifying the boundaries of your role can prevent misunderstandings and potential feelings of betrayal.

Encourage your mentee to seek additional perspectives, which not only broadens their support system but also demonstrates that you are not trying to control or monopolize their development. And always, steer clear of manipulative behaviors, even unintentionally. Mentorship is about empowering others, not wielding influence over them. If you find yourself giving directives rather than suggestions, or using your authority to suppress your mentee's autonomy, it's time to reassess your role in this relationship. Mentorship should be a space where mentees feel free to explore ideas, take risks, and learn from mistakes—not one where they feel dominated or stifled.

Avoid Morphing into the Mentor Monster

Fostering a healthy balance of power is crucial in any mentoring relationship. Encourage your mentee to voice concerns, ask questions, and challenge ideas without fear of retribution. This helps build a foundation of trust and mutual respect, empowering your mentee to grow confidently and independently. Being a good mentor means regularly checking your ego, focusing on your mentee's best interests, and creating a positive, growth-oriented environment.

In sum, mentoring is more than sharing knowledge—it's about helping your mentee grow authentically. By avoiding the pitfalls of malignant, mismatched, and missing mentors, you cultivate a relationship rooted in trust, growth, and mutual respect, ensuring both parties thrive.

Giving Back

As you've progressed through your own mentoring journey, the next step is to give back. With the new tools and insights you've developed, it's time to put them into practice not just for yourself, but for others. Think of yourself as a vector, a force with both magnitude and direction, who is capable of guiding and influencing those around you. Just as your mentors have done for you, now it's your turn to contribute where someone else may need support. Indeed, the person who needs your help the most might not reach out to you and might not even be able to articulate the kind of support they need. Be ready to intervene. Who in your network could benefit from a mentoring intervention, much like the way Geoff and Tim helped me? This is your opportunity to use your experiences and growth to become a positive force in someone else's development.

Are you asking yourself: Why me? Why are you now in a position to provide mentorship? Consider the unique strengths, experiences, and perspectives you bring to the table. We dedicated the earlier part of this book to convincing you that you are worthy of support from a network of mentoring relationships. Spotting someone who needs your guidance often involves looking for those in the same position you once were—unsure, facing new challenges, or tumbling through times of transition. Helping doesn't mean taking over or giving them all the answers, but instead, guiding them toward the tools and insights that will allow them to discover their own path and their own superpowers. Mentorship is about empowering others with the confidence to make their own informed decisions, just as you've learned to do throughout your own journey.

Good mentors are hard to find. Good mentees are too, as so many people who need the kind of help this book provides might be unaware or hesitant to seek the support they need. As you step into these roles, of peer and of mentor, reflect on the tools you've learned throughout this book. Think about the skills, frameworks, and strategies that have helped you grow. How can

Chapter 11: Growing Into a Mentor

you now use these to support and elevate someone else? Your mentoring relationships should be grounded in the same principles of growth and collaboration that shaped your experience. Whether you're sharing advice, offering feedback, or simply being a sounding board, you have a wealth of knowledge to pass on. Consider how you might adapt these tools for your protégé, helping them chart their own course, much like your mentors did for you.

As you've come to understand throughout this journey, it should be obvious you have a Superpower Portfolio and you are enough. Too often, we find ourselves in rooms with people who seem to have more—more experience, more connections, more confidence. The temptation to follow the popular advice of "fake it 'til you make it" can be strong. But don't fall for it. As consumer advocate Robert L. FitzPatrick aptly put it, that phrase is "inherently manipulative, deceptive, fraudulent, inauthentic." It's a mindset that has seeped into our culture, but it's not the path forward. Please, don't fake it. That's what imposters do. You are not an imposter.

Instead, embrace this truth. That is, "be it, and you'll see it." Be the person you've worked so hard to become, and in time, the rest will follow. It may not happen immediately, but it will happen—because you are the real thing. You've earned your place here, and you've built yourself through hard work and resilience. You own your origin story, your strengths, and your superpowers. That's what makes you authentic, capable, and ready to give back. Now go forth and mentor others and help them find that same belief in themselves, because the power of being real is something you've already mastered.

Let's Stay Connected

Thank you for taking the time to read this book. I hope it has inspired you to believe in yourself and your superpowers. Now it's time for you to take steps toward building the connections that empower your career and life.

I would love to stay in touch and hear your thoughts!

- **Connect on LinkedIn**: www.linkedin.com/in/davidaron

- **Visit my website/blog**: Mentorvention.com

- **Scan the QR codes below to connect with me instantly!**

LinkedIn

Website

On my website, you'll find additional resources, articles, and updates about mentoring, career development, and professional growth. You'll also be the first to know about new workshops, events, and tools designed to help you navigate your mentoring relationships.

www.ingramcontent.com/pod-product-compliance
Lightning Source LLC
Chambersburg PA
CBHW051822090426
42736CB00011B/1607